Overcoming Pakistan's Nuclear Dangers

Mark Fitzpatrick

Overcoming Pakistan's Nuclear Dangers

Mark Fitzpatrick

IISS The International Institute for Strategic Studies

The International Institute for Strategic Studies

Arundel House | 13–15 Arundel Street | Temple Place | London | WC2R 3DX | UK

First published March 2014 by **Routledge**
4 Park Square, Milton Park, Abingdon, Oxon, OX14 4RN

for **The International Institute for Strategic Studies**
Arundel House, 13–15 Arundel Street, Temple Place, London, WC2R 3DX, UK
www.iiss.org

Simultaneously published in the USA and Canada by **Routledge**
270 Madison Ave., New York, NY 10016

Routledge is an imprint of Taylor & Francis, an Informa Business

The International Institute for Strategic Studies is an independent centre for research, information and debate on the problems of conflict, however caused, that have, or potentially have, an important military content. The Council and Staff of the Institute are international and its membership is drawn from almost 100 countries. The Institute is independent and it alone decides what activities to conduct. It owes no allegiance to any government, any group of governments or any political or other organisation. The IISS stresses rigorous research with a forward-looking policy orientation and places particular emphasis on bringing new perspectives to the strategic debate.

The Institute's publications are designed to meet the needs of a wider audience than its own membership and are available on subscription, by mail order and in good bookshops. Further details at www.iiss.org.

Printed and bound in Great Britain by Bell & Bain Ltd, Thornliebank, Glasgow

British Library Cataloguing in Publication Data
A catalogue record for this book is available from the British Library

Library of Congress Cataloging in Publication Data

ADELPHI series
ISSN 1944-5571

ADELPHI 443
ISBN 978-1-138-79667-6

Contents

ACKNOWLEDGEMENTS

The author owes much to the year-long research assistance of Daniel Painter. This book was improved by helpful suggestions from Antoine Levesques, Shashank Joshi, Mansoor Ahmed, Rahul Roy-Chaudhury, Nigel Inkster, Toby Dalton, George Perkovich, Bruno Tertrais, Brian Cloughley, Adelphi editors Nick Redman and Mona Moussavi, and anonymous officials in three capitals. Julia Wacket provided helpful fact-checking and formatting assistance. Most of all, the author appreciates the forbearance of Kyoko, his wife, to whom this book is dedicated.

GLOSSARY AND ACRONYMS

BMD	ballistic-missile defence
CBM	confidence-building measure
CD	Conference on Disarmament
CHASNUPP	Chashma Nuclear Power Reactor
Counterforce	Targeting of an opponent's military forces.
Countervalue	Targeting of an opponent's valued assets, such as cities and civilian populations.
CTBT	Comprehensive Nuclear-Test-Ban Treaty
DRDO	Defence Research and Development Organisation
FBR	fast-breeder reactor. A reactor capable of generating (breeding) more fissile material than it consumes; called 'fast' because it does not use a moderator to slow down neutrons.
FMCT	Fissile Material Cut-off Treaty
Gas centrifuge enrichment	Enrichment process that involves spinning UF_6 gas in tubes to separate U-235 and U-238 isotopes.
Heavy-water reactor	Type of nuclear reactor that uses heavy water (deuterium oxide, D_2O) to help achieve fission.
HEU	highly enriched uranium
HuT	Hizb ut-Tahrir
IAEA	International Atomic Energy Agency
ICBM	intercontinental ballistic missile
IED	improvised explosive device
IPFM	International Panel on Fissile Material
ISI	Inter-Services Intelligence
JeM	Jaysh-e-Mohammad
JSOC	Joint Special Operations Command
KANUPP	Karachi Nuclear Power Plant
KRL	Khan Research Laboratories
LeT	Lashkar-e-Taiba
LoC	Line of Control. The military control line between Indian- and Pakistani-controlled areas of Kashmir, formerly known as the ceasefire line after the Indo-Pakistani War of 1947–48.
MAD	Mutual Assured Destruction
MIRV	multiple independently targetable re-entry vehicle

MRBM	medium-range ballistic missile
MWe	megawatt electrical
MWt	megawatt thermal
NCA	National Command Authority
NPT	Nuclear Non-Proliferation Treaty
NSG	Nuclear Suppliers Group
P-2, P-3, P-4	second-, third- and fourth-generation centrifuge models
PAEC	Pakistan Atomic Energy Commission
PAL	permissive action link. A sophisticated lock designed to prevent accidental or unauthorised launching of nuclear weapons.
PARR	Pakistan Atomic Research Reactor
PINSTECH	Pakistan Institute of Nuclear Sciences and Technology
Reprocessing	Process of separating plutonium from spent reactor fuel.
SPD	Strategic Plans Division
SRBM	short-range ballistic missile
Sub-kiloton weapon	Weapon with a yield equivalent to less than 1,000 tonnes of TNT.
SWU	separative work unit. A measure of work expended in the enrichment process, used to quantify centrifuge output.
TEL	transporter-erector launcher
TNW	tactical nuclear weapon. A weapon with a short range and small size that is designed for use on a battlefield, in contrast to strategic weapons designed for use against cities, bases and other larger-area targets with the intention of impeding the enemy's ability and will to wage war.
TTP	Tehrik-e-Taliban Pakistan
UF$_6$	uranium hexafluoride
Uranium-235 (U-235) content	Percentage of the fissile U-235 isotope. Natural uranium contains 0.7% U-235; enriched uranium has a larger percentage; and depleted uranium (a by-product of enrichment) has less than 0.7%.
Uranium conversion	Conversion of yellowcake into uranium compounds used for enrichment (UF$_6$) and fuel fabrication (UO$_2$).
Uranium enrichment	Process of increasing the percentage of U-235 relative to U-238; low enriched uranium (LEU) is required for light-water reactors, highly enriched uranium (HEU) is required for nuclear weapons.
UTN	Ummah Tameer-e-Nau

Nuclear specialists are often asked which country presents the greatest source of concern. One might say Russia, because it holds the largest inventory of nuclear weapons (followed closely by the United States) and because, together with other former Soviet republics, it is the source of the greatest amount of trafficked nuclear material. One could point to China, because it has the fastest-growing nuclear industry and because it is the least transparent among the five declared nuclear-weapons states. North Korea is often put at the top of the list because of its nuclear threats and propensity for provocation. Meanwhile, the most media attention has been focused on Iran because of its growing nuclear capabilities in defiance of United Nations Security Council resolutions.

For many experts, however, the answer is Pakistan. Nowhere is there a greater potential nexus between nuclear proliferation and terrorism. Pakistan has both the world's fastest-growing nuclear arsenal and the largest concentration of groups bent on acts of terrorism. Growing fundamentalism, ethnic violence, weak political institutions and a fragile economy combine to raise questions about the very security of the state and thus the security of its nuclear crown jewels. Pakistan is often seen to have the world's worst record of nuclear stewardship,[1] having allowed, and in some cases assisted, the sale of its nuclear-weapons related technology to at least three so-called 'rogue states'. As explained in Chapter Five, Pakistan nuclear metallurgist Abdul Qadeer Khan transferred uranium-enrichment equipment and know-how to North Korea, Iran and Libya, and attempted to sell them to Iraq. US arms-control expert Joseph Cirincione put it baldly: 'Pakistan is the most dangerous country on Earth,' with South Asia the region most likely to experience nuclear combat.[2] US President Barack Obama reportedly told aides once that it was Pakistan that worried him the most.[3]

Yet Western leaders rarely fret publicly about the security of Pakistan's nuclear arsenal. There is good reason not to. Pakistan is a partner of the US in the once-labelled 'war on terrorism', and a 'major non-NATO ally', a designation shared with only 14 other countries. It is impolite to speak ill of one's friends. There is also a strong policy imperative to keeping discreet: public expressions of concern can be counter-productive. Foreign expressions of concern about nuclear dangers in Pakistan are interpreted there to mean censure and censure is met with determined resistance. Brig. (Retd) Feroz Khan, a US-based national-security expert who once headed the arms-control unit of the Strategic Plans Division of the Pakistani military, writes that 'the more assiduously the [nuclear] program was opposed by India and the West, the more precious it became. It evolved into the most significant symbol of national determination and a central element of Pakistan's identity.'[4] Thus from the US president on down through the ranks of US military and civilian officials, the common refrain is an expression of confidence in Pakistan's nuclear security.[5]

These expressions of reassurance are at sharp variance with the popular view in Pakistan, where most citizens believe the

United States seeks to denude the country of its nuclear arsenal. Western expressions of concern about Pakistani nuclear security, especially when coupled with talk of Pakistan as a failing state, are misinterpreted as proof of this desire. The May 2011 raid in which US Navy SEALs penetrated deep into Pakistan to kill Osama bin Laden and remove his body was widely seen in Pakistan as a practice run to extract their nuclear weapons. Given the population's deep anti-Americanism and proclivity to conspiracy theories, it takes little to fan the flames of paranoia.

Western non-governmental experts who write about proliferation and terrorism are sometimes seen as part of the supposed foreign conspiracy. Yet academic integrity argues for candour. How though to analyse Pakistan's nuclear issues in a way that does not make things worse? The constructive answer is to combine intellectual honesty with fairness to Pakistan's position. Like a previous volume on Pakistan's nuclear programme edited by the current author,[6] this book is informed by Pakistani perspectives on the steps taken to reduce nuclear risks. The analysis has benefitted from several discussions with Pakistani officials, including at the highest levels of the strategic establishment, although the assessments, naturally, are the author's own.

Pakistani officials would surely prefer that this book address not only their country's nuclear posture but also India's. Pakistan's nuclear-weapons programme, based as it is on the perceived Indian threat, cannot be adequately discussed outside the bilateral context. India thus features prominently in many of the chapters, particularly those dealing with the potential for a nuclear exchange in South Asia, the motivations behind Pakistan's growing arsenal and the nuclear-arms competition. Yet several of the concerns posed by Pakistan's nuclear programme do not have a bilateral context. India did not spark Pakistan's transfer of nuclear technology. Nor does India have a direct role regarding the dangers of nuclear terrorism or the potential for nuclear accidents.

Solutions to the set of dangers surrounding Pakistan's nuclear programme will necessarily involve India, both directly and indirectly. Western powers will also have a major role to play. As argued in the final chapter, they should be ready to recognise Pakistan as a normal nuclear state and to offer nuclear cooperation, if it adopts policies associated with responsible nuclear behaviour.

Notes

1 China actually had a worse record. In the 1980s, it transferred 50kg of weapons-ready highly enriched uranium to Pakistan, as well as a weapons design. China also reportedly assisted nuclear-weapons programmes in Argentina, Brazil and Iran and possibly other states. Pakistan's proliferation record is usually considered in a harsher light because of the more recent timeline and the heightened media attention to its deeds.

2 Joseph Cirincione, 'The Most Dangerous Country on Earth', *Georgetown Journal of International Affairs*, Summer/Fall 2013, pp. 91–100.

3 David E. Sanger, *Confront and Conceal: Obama's Secret Wars and Surprising Use of American Power* (New York: Broadway Books, 2012), p. 132.

4 Feroz Khan, *Eating Grass: The Making of the Pakistani Bomb* (Stanford, CA: Stanford University Press, 2012), p. 2.

5 Paul Kerr and Mary Beth Nikitin, 'Pakistan's Nuclear Weapons: Proliferation and Security Issues', Congressional Research Service, 13 February 2013, http://www.fas.org/sgp/crs/nuke/RL34248.pdf.

6 International Institute for Strategic Studies (IISS), *Nuclear Black Markets: Pakistan, A.Q. Khan and the rise of proliferation networks – A net assessment* (London: IISS, 2007).

CHAPTER ONE

Pakistan's nuclear programme

In the past few years, Pakistan's nuclear arsenal and strategy have undergone dramatic changes. The first generation of the arsenal consisted of a small number of free-fall weapons based on highly enriched uranium (HEU). Today, Pakistan has moved to plutonium-based weapons that are deliverable by nine different ballistic- and cruise-missile systems and provide options for battlefield use. The latter capability has lowered the nuclear threshold.

Beginnings

Pakistan's nuclear endeavours began with peaceful intentions. In 1955, it was one of the first countries to take advantage of US President Dwight D. Eisenhower's 'Atoms for Peace' programme, signing an agreement for cooperation on the peaceful use of nuclear energy. The Pakistan Atomic Energy Commission (PAEC) was established in 1956 and soon after, hundreds of students were sent overseas for training in nuclear-related fields. In 1963, the Pakistan Institute of Nuclear Sciences and Technology (PINSTECH) was established near Rawalpindi. The United States supplied a 5MWt[1] (megawatt, thermal) civilian research reactor, called PARR-1 (Pakistan Atomic Research Reactor), which went critical in 1965, using 93% HEU fuel. Later it was converted to run on 19.75% enriched uranium fuel and upgraded to 10MWt. In 1972, Pakistan inaugurated a Canadian-supplied nuclear power plant, the 137MWe KANUPP-1 (Karachi Nuclear Power Plant). In 1989, China provided a very small 27kW (kilowatt) research reactor, PARR-2. All three reactors were put under safeguards by the International Atomic Energy Agency (IAEA) under a facility-specific agreement to ensure they would be kept to civilian use.

As minister of mineral resources from 1958 to 1962, Zulfiqar Ali Bhutto was a strong supporter of the civilian programme, but he soon came to advocate that Pakistan should also harness nuclear technology for military purposes. Fear of domination by India, distrust of the US alliance and concern that growing international interest in a treaty to ban the spread of nuclear weapons would close the door on Pakistan's options were among his motivations.[2] In 1964, when China first tested a nuclear weapon, Bhutto, who by then was foreign minister, concluded that India would also go nuclear and that Pakistan would therefore need to as well. In March the next year, as the 1965 India–Pakistan War began to heat up, he famously declared in an interview with the *Manchester Guardian* that 'if India makes an atom bomb, then even if we have to feed on grass and leaves – or even if we have to starve – we shall also produce an atom bomb as we would be left with no other alternative.'[3]

The timeline is significant. Contrary to popular belief that India's nuclear programme stimulated Pakistan to follow the same path, Bhutto began lobbying for nuclear weapons before there was conclusive evidence that India would have the bomb. He was correct, of course, in anticipating India's path but it was not initially an action–reaction sequence. Rather, he

Map 1. **Pakistan's nuclear facilities**

was acting on expectations, a pattern that would be repeated in the unfolding of Pakistan's nuclear history. And as with later events, the US role was significant. As Bhutto makes clear in a monograph he wrote in 1967, the deterioration of US–Pakistan relations was a major factor in his quest for a nuclear deterrent.[4] He was particularly bitter about Washington's failure to come to Pakistan's aid in the 1965 war, as he contended had been guaranteed, and about US economic support for India. He also argued that if Washington's extended deterrence was not good enough for France, it should not be relied upon by Pakistan either. In December 1965, however, President Ayub Khan rejected the idea of pursuing unsafeguarded sensitive nuclear technologies, claiming that Pakistan could buy a bomb off the shelf if it was ever needed.[5]

In 1971, after Pakistan suffered a humiliating defeat to India and the loss of its eastern half (now Bangladesh), and after Bhutto became president, an early priority was to put his nuclear disposition into practice. At a meeting in Multan in January 1972, he asked a group of scientists and officials – unrealistically – to produce a weapon in five years' time. US-trained scientist Munir Ahmad Khan was put in charge of PAEC to oversee the development.

India's first nuclear test in March 1974 gave urgency to the project and the next month a cabinet meeting confirmed a decision to build nuclear weapons, transforming what until then had been seen as a hedging option.[6] PAEC pursued both paths to a nuclear weapon: plutonium via reprocessing spent reactor fuel and HEU.

The uranium path was boosted when A.Q. Khan, then working at a Dutch company connected to the Urenco uranium-enrichment consortium, wrote to Bhutto in September 1974 offering his services. A year later the metallurgist returned to Pakistan with stolen designs of gas centrifuges. He initially was put to work in PAEC, but clashes with M.A. Khan led to Bhutto assigning him full control over the centrifuge project in his own laboratory at Kahuta, later named the Khan Research Laboratories.[7] By April 1984, A.Q. Khan announced the production of HEU, and eight months later said in a promotional video that Pakistan was in a position to detonate a nuclear device 'on a week's notice'.[8] This was probably an exaggeration given that the centrifuge project was marred by technical difficulties and three major earthquakes had destroyed thousands of machines.[9] Meanwhile, on 11 March 1983 PAEC had conducted the first of 24 cold tests of a nuclear device at Kirana Hills in central Punjab.[10] In 1986, a US National Intelligence Estimate concluded that Pakistan was only 'two screwdriver turns' from assembling a weapon and could do so within two weeks of making a decision.[11] The earliest credible report of weapons assembly, however, did not come until the 1990 Kashmir conflict.

Uranium enrichment

Until recently, uranium enrichment was the mainstay of Pakistan's nuclear-weapons programme, while the plutonium infrastructure lay dormant for want of unsafeguarded spent fuel for reprocessing until the completion of the Khushab-1 reactor in 1997 and its commissioning in the following April. The nuclear devices detonated in May 1998 were widely assessed to have used HEU. Pakistan announced that five tests were conducted on 28 May – the same number that India had tested two weeks earlier – two with yields of 25kt and 15kt respectively, and three sub-kiloton tactical devices. The tests generated only one seismic signal, however, which indicated a total yield of 6–13kt. According to Feroz Khan, only one real bomb was exploded, while four other bomb designs were tested 'with triggers and natural uranium'.[12]

An additional test on 30 May at a separate location had a claimed yield of 18–20kt.[13] International experts assessed a much lower yield of 2–8kt, which suggests a fizzle, although it was claimed to be a miniaturised device.[14] According to some reports, including an initial air-sample analysis by the US Los Alamos National Laboratory, the 30 May test was of a plutonium device, although it is unknown where Pakistan could have obtained and separated the plutonium before secret facilities for this purpose were fully operational.[15] What fissile material was used in that test is relevant today in terms of the credibility of Pakistan's battlefield-use nuclear weapons.

Pakistan's enrichment capacity and stockpile are state secrets. Production capacity is estimated to be approximately 100kg of weapons-grade (90%) HEU a year,[16] but may be up to 180kg per year, according to some estimates.[17] Assuming that Pakistan's warheads each require 15–20kg of HEU,[18] that is enough for 5–7 weapons per year, but possibly up to 12. Production sufficient for six weapons per year is a reasonable estimate.

The HEU production estimates vary depending on assumptions about the type of centrifuge employed, for example to what extent the second-generation (P-2) designs that A.Q. Khan stole from the Netherlands are supplemented by more advanced P-3 and P-4 models.[19] According to eminent Pakistani physicist Pervez Hoodbhoy, at least a few thousand of the more advanced models must be in operation by now, hence the yearly HEU production rate can be expected to be several times larger than in the mid-1980s when Kahuta began operating.[20] In addition to Kahuta, smaller enrichment facilities were set up as research and development (R&D) or pilot plants at Gadwal, Sihala and Golra, all located 20–30km from Islamabad,[21] although they probably do not add significantly to the HEU production taking place at Kahuta.

A significant expansion of Pakistan's enrichment production would require complementary expansion of uranium hexafluoride (UF_6) feedstock production. In 2009, commercial satellite imagery appeared to show an expansion of the uranium-conversion facilities at Dera Ghazi Khan.[22] Pakistani scholar Mansoor Ahmed argues that the purpose of any such expansion would be to increase production of uranium oxide for fabricating natural (un-enriched) uranium fuel for new Khushab reactors.[23] He notes that the complex at Dera Ghazi

Khan is reported to have an annual production capacity of at least 200 tonnes of UF_6 – enough for 15,000–20,000 separative work units (SWU) per year.[24] This would be insufficient for the up to 45,000 SWU per year posited as an upper bound by the International Panel on Fissile Materials.[25]

By the end of 2012, the International Panel on Fissile Material estimated Pakistan's total production of HEU to be around 3 tonnes, plus or minus 1.2 tonnes.[26] Assuming 15–20kg is used for each bomb, this translates to a wide estimate of 90–280 weapons. As noted below, most analysts favour the low end of this range.

Plutonium production

As A.Q. Khan perfected enrichment, PAEC, in competition, continued work on plutonium. With assistance from several European companies, PAEC constructed the New Labs pilot plant for reprocessing at the PINSTECH complex which became operational in the early 1980s. To produce plutonium away from the eyes of the IAEA, PAEC in 1986 began constructing a heavy-water moderated 50MWt reactor at Khushab with Chinese assistance. The unsafeguarded reactor, which went critical in 1998, can produce 6–12kg of plutonium per year.[27] A second, similarly sized reactor at Khushab was begun between 2000 and 2002[28] and started operation in late 2009 or early 2010. In 2000, the New Labs facility began separating the plutonium from Khushab-1. Current annual production of separated plutonium is estimated to be about 12–24kg, enough for 2–5 weapons, assuming each requires 5–6kg.[29] At the beginning of 2013, Pakistan was assessed to have a stockpile of 100–200kg of plutonium, enough for 16–40 weapons.[30]

Within the last decade, Pakistan has been putting greater effort into expanding its plutonium-production capabilities. A third plutonium-production reactor at Khushab, which was begun in 2006, appears to be operational.[31] A fourth reactor, under construction since 2011, may begin production by 2015. The larger size of their cooling towers suggests to some analysts that Khushab-2 and -3 are respectively 35% and 65% larger than Khushab-1 in terms of thermal capacity (66MWt and 81MWt respectively).[32] There may be other explanations for the larger cooling towers.[33] Khushab-4 is probably at least the same size as Khushab-3. Together, the four reactors will be able to produce roughly 64kg of plutonium a year, enough for 10–12 plutonium weapons.

To reprocess this increased plutonium production, Pakistan has resumed construction of a large reprocessing plant at Chashma, near Khushab, most of which was built by France before it pulled out of the project in 1978.[34] Another new reprocessing plant is presumed to be under construction next to the existing one at the New Labs facility[35] or that plant's capacity might have been doubled.

Warheads

In addition to free-fall bomb models prepared by PAEC, Pakistan obtained a tested design from China of a 15–25kt HEU implosion-type warhead that is capable of delivery by either aircraft or missiles. This was the design that A.Q. Khan sold to Libya in 2001–02 for a warhead weighing about 500kg and measuring about 90cm in diameter. Foreign investigation of the Khan network later uncovered the existence of two other sophisticated designs for smaller, lighter and more powerful warheads than the first design from China.[36] According to two former US weapons designers, China also assisted by testing a Pakistani weapon design in 1990 with a yield of 10–12kt, although this is not confirmed.[37]

Given its expansion in plutonium production, for the past several years, Pakistan has been considered to have the fastest-growing nuclear-weapons programme in the world.[38] For eight years after the 1998 test, Pakistan's nuclear arsenal was assessed to have expanded by six weapons annually. Beginning in 2007, ten weapons a year were assumed to have been added.[39] With reprocessing of spent fuel from the third Khushab reactor, the estimate increases to about 13 weapons a year. By about 2016, after the fourth Khushab reactor comes online, the annual production could reach 16 or more.

Bruce Riedel, a former CIA analyst who served in the US National Security Council, judges that if it has not done so already, Pakistan's nuclear arsenal will soon surpass that of the United Kingdom,[40] which has no more than 225 weapons and will reduce this number to 180 by the mid-2020s. According to Riedel, Pakistan is even on course to become the fourth-largest nuclear-weapons state, ahead of France,[41] which is deemed to have 300 weapons.

All published estimates of Pakistan's nuclear arsenal are notional; nobody outside a select group within the nation's nuclear establishment knows for certain. Most estimates are based on assumptions about the amount of HEU and separated plutonium used for each weapon, the amount of fissile material produced and the amount converted into weapon cores, taking into account that perhaps 30% of the fissile material is held up in the production pipeline or is otherwise not immediately available for weapons purposes.[42] Washington-based nuclear-weapons specialists Hans Kristensen and Robert Norris estimate that in late 2010, Islamabad had enough fissile material for 160–249 warheads.[43] Fissile material is not the only constraining factor, however. There may be limits to Pakistan's capacity for converting highly enriched UF_6 to metal, and for producing and fabricating the 2,000 parts that comprise nuclear weapons.[44] The number of nuclear-capable launch vehicles is sometimes also considered when deriving arsenal estimates.

The most reliable expert sources assess that as of 2013, Pakistan had about 100–120 nuclear weapons. This is the range provided by the Stockholm International Peace Research Institute for its *Yearbook 2013*, which increased the estimate by ten over the previous year. As of 2014, the arsenal numbers about 110–130. It is possible, however, to calculate a number twice this size.

Pakistan could increase its bomb output by perhaps 60% above typical estimates if a composite core is used, combining a 2–3kg plutonium sphere surrounded by an HEU shell.[45] It is not known if Pakistan uses such a weapons design, but according to Hoodbhoy there is little doubt that Pakistan is seeking to do so. He notes that a plasma-physics group at PAEC has long researched fusion-weapon matters, albeit with little apparent progress.[46]

A caveat is needed here, however. Pakistan's nuclear arsenal will not grow inexorably along an upward trajectory. One reason is because the nation has limited sources of uranium ore. Since 2003, Pakistan's uranium-ore production has remained stable at 40 tonnes per year. This is sufficient to provide fuel for natural uranium-fuelled reactors with a capacity of about 150MWt or three of the Khushab-1-sized plants.[47] But the HEU programme also needs uranium ore. Given these requirements, Ahmed estimates that at current production levels, and unless fresh reserves begin production, the ore might be exhausted by 2020.[48] It could happen even sooner if the newer Khushab reactors are larger than the first one.

Pakistan cannot easily import more uranium because, unlike India, it has been denied an exception to Nuclear Suppliers Group (NSG) guidelines that prohibit nuclear cooperation with non-adherents to the Nuclear Non-Proliferation Treaty (NPT). The enriched uranium fuel that Pakistan receives from China under a grandfathered agreement can only be used in civilian reactors. A high-priority search for additional uranium deposits appears to have produced more media hype than actual results.

Even if no other uranium deposits are discovered, there are three other potential sources of uranium. The easiest source is in the depleted uranium tails from Pakistan's enrichment programme to date. The tails contain about 0.2–0.3% U-235 content. Uranium with a U-235 content of about 0.6% is also available in the spent fuel from military reactors and, at lower enrichment levels, in spent fuel from power reactors. The uranium could be separated using existing reprocessing facilities. A third possibility is the extraction of uranium from rock phosphate, which is removed anyway when di-ammonium phosphate is produced for fertiliser. Pakistan has been producing this fertiliser since 1999 and freely imports phosphoric acid from Morocco.[49] Although extracting uranium in this manner is not economical for commercial ventures, it may suffice for military purposes. Whether any or all of these methods would produce enough uranium for a further expansion in Pakistan's fissile-material production is unclear.

In addition to constraints imposed by the availability of uranium, the size of the arsenal will depend on perceived needs, which can change. Although Pakistan insists that it is not necessary to match India 'weapon for weapon', the size and composition of India's arsenal are significant factors in Pakistan's strategic plans. Pakistani officials have occasionally posited that India aims to acquire 400 nuclear weapons.[50] In 2004, an Indian Ministry of Defence official was quoted as saying that India in the next 5–7 years would have 300–400 fission and thermonuclear weapons distributed to air, sea and land forces.[51] Apart from that unscripted remark by an unnamed official, India has never assigned a specific number to its nuclear policy of credible minimum deterrence. Nor has

Pakistan. The nation's official line is that it needs only enough to deter India. It is doubtful that Pakistan would feel the need for 400 for this purpose, even if India were judged to have that many. The number depends on targeting requirements. American arms-control expert Michael Krepon concludes that at present, the nuclear requirements emphasise credibility over minimalism. The stockpile will likely continue to expand as long as the programme is seen as successful, relations with India remain contentious and Pakistan's sense of international isolation worsens.[52]

According to a senior Pakistani official, by about 2020, pluto-nium production may be adequate for its defence purposes, although those requirements could change depending on the international environment.[53] Ahmed contends that if uranium-ore limits are reached in 2020, it would impose an upper limit of about 200–250 weapons.[54] Similarly, a senior Pakistani official told a European scholar: 'if China doesn't need more than 200–250 weapons, why should we?'[55]

Delivery systems

The first nuclear weapons were developed for delivery by F-16 A/B model fighter aircraft purchased from the US that were modified indigenously to be nuclear capable. In addition to the F-16s, Pakistan reportedly modified *Mirage*-V fighters from France for use in nuclear missions as well as recently acquired Chinese JF-17 *Thunder* fighters (replacing Chinese A-5 fighters).

When US legislation threatened to cut off military sales over the nuclear programme, Pakistan turned to China and North Korea for ballistic-missile cooperation. Starting in 1988, China supplied the 250–300km-range solid-fuelled M-11 missile, which Pakistan called *Ghaznavi* (after an eleventh-century Afghan conqueror) or *Hatf*-III,[56] and the 700km-range solid-fuelled M-9, which Pakistan named *Hatf*-IV (or *Shaheen* meaning falcon). In 1993, a deal was struck with North Korea to obtain the liquid-fuelled 1,200km-range *Nodong*, which was renamed *Ghauri* (after a twelfth-century Muslim ruler) or *Hatf*-V.

Pakistan today gives priority to solid-fuelled missiles, which are easier to transport and faster to launch. In 2012, the range of the *Shaheen* was extended to over 1,000km. Under development is the *Shaheen*-2 (*Hatf*-VI) missile with a range of 2,000–2,500km, which would bring all of India's major cities within range. It is seen as the mainstay of the nation's future deterrent.[57]

A new missile system that has caused alarm in Western capitals has a far shorter reach. On 19 April 2011, Pakistan announced the successful test of a 60km-range artillery-launched short-range ballistic missile (SRBM) identified as *Hatf*-IX (or *Nasr*, meaning victory). It was tested again in May 2012, February 2013 and November 2013. Designed for battle-field use, the solid-fuelled missile is carried by a multi-tube transporter-erector launcher (TEL) that is also used for some conventional multi-launch rocket systems.[58] The missile has an apparent diameter of about 361mm, meaning it is able to fire rockets with a diameter of 350mm.[59] It can carry both conventional high-explosive warheads and boosted-fission nuclear devices.[60]

Another solid-fuelled SRBM, the *Hatf*-II (or *Abdali*, named after an eighteenth-century Afghan king), with a range of 180km, is also designed to fire both conventional and nuclear weapons. It was first flight-tested in 2002, but the dual-use purpose was not claimed until the second test in 2003.[61] It is 560mm in diameter and can carry a warhead up to 500kg. The missile was tested again in 2005, 2006, 2007, 2011, 2012 and 2013. A press release after the March 2012 test said the *Abdali* 'provides an operational level capability to Pakistan's Strategic Forces, additional to the strategic and tactical level capability, which Pakistan already possesses'.[62]

Pakistan is also developing nuclear-capable cruise missiles: the 500–700km-range ground-launched *Hatf*-VII (or *Babur*, named after the first Mughal emperor) and the 350km-range air-launched *Hatf*-VIII (or *Ra'ad*, meaning thunder), both with a fuselage diameter of 520mm. According to press releases, these are low-flying, terrain-hugging missiles that can deliver both nuclear and conventional warheads with pinpoint accuracy.[63] Air- and sea-launched versions of the *Babur* are also planned.[64]

Although a sea-launched *Babur* could not threaten New Delhi, which is beyond its range, such a system would give Pakistan a more reliable second-strike capability. Indeed, the military describes the Naval Strategic Force Command as the 'custodian of the nation's 2nd strike capability'.[65] The *Babur* missiles would likely be deployed in Pakistan's five *Agosta*-class submarines, which were acquired from France and are currently equipped with anti-ship *Exocet* missiles. Pakistan may also intend to deploy nuclear cruise missiles on new diesel-electric submarines that are supposedly to be purchased from China.[66] However, China itself does not yet field a credible submarine-launched nuclear missile. Some analysts argue that Pakistan does not have the budget to bring the desired triad to fruition.[67]

Whether Pakistan has reliable nuclear weapons for the short-range systems is a matter of some doubt among outside observers. Nuclear weapons small enough for these missiles would probably need to use a plutonium core and it is generally assumed that the complexity of such devices requires testing for assured reliability.[68] As noted above, it is also believed that Pakistan has never tested a plutonium weapon. One possible answer may be that Chinese HEU bomb-design assistance to Pakistan was complemented by a design for a small plutonium bomb, although there is no evidence of such a transfer. A more likely possibility, advocated by Pakistani analysts, is that 20 years of sub-critical cold tests of small plutonium bombs have given the Pakistan military sufficient confidence to introduce the systems without hot testing.[69] India chooses not to believe it and so portrays disinterest in the *Nasr*.[70] But India cannot assume that Pakistan's plutonium warheads would not work. As far as is known, every nuclear-armed country has succeeded in producing a fissile reaction in its first nuclear test.

Nuclear policy

Believing that declared doctrines are nothing but 'verbal posturing' meant only for diplomatic argumentation,[71] Pakistan has not publicly proclaimed a nuclear doctrine as such. Yet on the basis of Strategic Plans Division (SPD) briefings to select visitors and articles by SPD officials, the central tenets of its nuclear posture are clear. Krepon identifies four: an India-specific focus; minimum credible deterrence; readiness to employ against conventional attack; and dynamic strategic requirements.[72]

India specific

Pakistan's stated policy is 'to deter all forms of external aggression'. Like all nuclear powers, Pakistan insists that its nuclear weapons are for defensive purposes. An SPD briefing to a team from the International Institute for Strategic Studies (IISS) in 2013 asserted that 'nuclear weapons are solely for deterrence against aggression, and if deterrence breaks down, then for the defence of sovereignty.'[73]

On occasion, Pakistani officials have spoken about deterring Israel and even the United States.[74] Yet the motivations behind Pakistan's policy are entirely India-specific. Every aspect of Pakistan's nuclear posture has been conceived with that potential aggressor in mind. The first clear exposition of Pakistan's nuclear doctrine, authored by three former officials in October 1999 and surely cleared by the bureaucracy, was written in response to a draft India nuclear doctrine, for example.[75] More recently, SPD Arms Control and Disarmament head Khalid Banuri characterised Pakistan's nuclear arsenal as designed 'to deny India the space for launching any kind of aggression against Pakistan'.[76]

Minimum credible deterrence

'Minimum credible deterrence' has been the slogan since the early days of Pakistan's nuclear programme. The catchphrase itself is a take-off of India's 'credible minimum deterrence', in both cases without a comma, meaning that the first adjective modifies the second. Pakistan inverted the first two words, not just to be different but also to put greater emphasis on the need for credibility. What constitutes 'minimum credible deterrence' is left unstated, other than that it 'cannot be quantified in static numbers'.[77]

To buttress the claim concerning minimalism, Pakistani officials point to their unrequited pursuit of a 'strategic restraint regime' (SRR). This concept stems from the aftermath of the 1998 nuclear tests, when the United States engaged India and Pakistan in an intense eight-month period of bilateral dialogues, urging strategic restraint. Washington advocated adoption of a 'minimum deterrence posture', including the establishment of a finite ceiling for fissile-material production. Other elements included: geographical separation of major components of nuclear arsenals and delivery means; the segregation of delivery systems from warhead locations; and declaring non-nuclear delivery systems with their specific locations. Although neither interlocutor accepted what was referred to as a 'strategic pause', Pakistan put forward its own SRR proposal, matching the principle of nuclear restraint with conventional-force restraint.[78] India has never been interested in talks that would address both strategic and conventional forces.

Credibility depends both on possessing reliable nuclear weapons and projecting the will to use them to inflict unacceptable damage. Thus, Pakistani leaders, more often than their Indian counterparts, speak publicly about their nuclear deterrence.[79] President Pervez Musharraf claimed in 2005 that Pakistan had reached the minimum-deterrence level.[80] As French strategic expert Bruno Tertrais notes, this bold statement probably referred to an initial capability to reliably hit a few Indian cities.[81]

The priority attached to credibility over minimalism has accelerated in recent years, as described in the section above on the growing arsenal and fissile-material production capabilities, and the introduction of battlefield-use strategic weapons. The word 'minimum' was even dropped in one press release in December 2010.[82] It might be noted that India also emphasises credibility over minimalism.[83] Those in charge of Pakistan's nuclear forces recognise the need for limits. They insist, therefore, that one of the first elements of their nuclear posture is the 'maintenance of adequate forces within national resources constraints and avoidance of a costly arms race'.[84]

Allowing for first use

Rejecting notions of 'no first use',[85] Pakistan reserves the right to use nuclear weapons against conventional attack. Indeed, this is the basic premise of Pakistan's nuclear posture. Facing a potential enemy at whose hands it has three times suffered defeat and whose conventional superiority grows ever greater, Pakistan sees nuclear weapons as an equaliser. Pakistani officials also place no credence in India's declared no-first-use doctrine. They assume that India would employ nuclear weapons if it judged vital national interests to be at stake. In fact, India qualified its no-first-use policy in 2003, allowing for use in response to a major attack by biological or chemical weapons.

Pakistan does say that it will not 'use or threat[en] to use nuclear weapons against any non-nuclear weapons state – unless that state joins a hostile military coalition and nuclear-armed state(s)'.[86] Pakistan has also said that while it does not subscribe to a no-first-use policy, it does subscribe to 'no first use of force', as required under the UN Charter.[87]

Under what circumstances Pakistan would use nuclear weapons is left deliberately vague. Pakistani officials fear that drawing too clear a red line would embolden Indian action just short of the threshold.[88] In the years immediately after Pakistan's nuclear test, national leaders said that the weapons would be used only if 'national integrity' or the existence of the state were threatened.[89] Two Italian disarmament experts who met with SPD head Lt.-Gen. Khalid Kidwai in January 2001, during a tense period of confrontation at the Line of Control after the December 2001 assault on the Indian parliament, published his reported characterisation of four thresholds for nuclear use. Frequently referred to in other works on Pakistan's nuclear programme, Kidwai said that in case deterrence fails, nuclear weapons would be used if:

a. 'India attacks Pakistan and conquers a large part of its territory (space threshold);
b. India destroys a large part either of its land or air forces (military threshold);
c. India proceeds to the economic strangling of Pakistan (economic strangling), including a naval blockade or blocking the Indus River;
d. India pushes Pakistan into political destabilization or creates a large scale internal subversion in Pakistan (domestic destabilization).'[90]

Insisting that it was not an attempt at nuclear signalling, Pakistani officials explain that the 'plausible' thresholds are indicative and should not be viewed in isolation from one another.[91] Krepon notes that most of these thresholds are relics of Pakistan's past wars with India and have little relevance to current circumstances. He concludes that the most likely threshold for nuclear use would be significant losses of Pakistani combat aircraft.[92] The space threshold is also relevant, but here the threshold is probably much less than 'a large part' of Pakistan's territory. Most analysts assess that the threshold could be as low as an Indian advancement to Pakistan's lifeline in the Indus Valley, which lies 50–190km into Pakistani territory. Based on Pakistani rhetoric, it is conceivable that even a lesser incursion could provoke nuclear retaliation by Pakistan. A purposeful ambiguity concerning its red line for use of low-yield nuclear weapons is intended to complicate the cost-benefit analysis of any of India's options.

In response to the Indian Army's supposed plans for waging a conventional war under the nuclear threshold, Pakistan has lowered that threshold. It is not clear whether the purpose of using battlefield nuclear weapons would be to slow or halt advancing Indian forces or, rather, to send a political signal. Nor has Pakistan indicated whether it would employ nuclear weapons in the event of an Indian precision conventional attack against targets in Pakistan associated with violent jihadist groups, in retaliation for terrorist attacks by them in India.

Dynamic strategic requirements

Strategic requirements are dynamic, depending on changes in the perceived threat posed by India. Pakistan's military and civilian leaders have never said publicly or, as far as can be known, even privately what the requirements are. They say only that they depend on the evolving nature of the threat. The threat, of course, is in the eyes of the beholder. Although analysts discern little aggressive intent on India's part, Pakistani strategists see a less benign neighbour. Their threat perceptions are focused largely on India's capabilities and an often selective reading of Indian statements. India's strategic requirements are not static either, especially in light of China's growing military might. Dynamic strategic postures in all three countries create mutually reinforcing threat perceptions and a spiralling arms competition.

India's growing conventional military capabilities, as much as its nuclear assets, affect Pakistan's strategic requirements. In 2008, Peter Lavoy, American scholar and later Pentagon official on South Asia strategic issues, wrote that Indian advances in intelligence, surveillance and precision targeting that enabled it to locate and destroy strategic targets could prompt Pakistan to lower its nuclear threshold.[93] A Pakistan foreign ministry spokesman made the same point: 'There are acquisitions of sophisticated weaponry by our neighbour which will disturb the conventional balance between our two countries and hence, lower the nuclear threshold.'[94] Pakistani Brigadier Khawar Hanif put it this way: 'The wider the conventional asymmetry, the lower the nuclear threshold.'[95]

In addition to the move away from minimalism, the growth of Pakistan's nuclear arsenal reflects an evolution of its strategic doctrine. For the first decade after Pakistan became a nuclear power, the deterrence strategy was based entirely on countervalue strikes against Indian cities. Today, Pakistan has both countervalue and counterforce nuclear options. Writing in an academic capacity, SPD Arms Control and Disarmament Director Adil Sultan terms the evolving nuclear strategy 'flexible deterrence options', which he says aims for a proportionate response, rather than massive retaliation against India.[96] Pakistani officials, including Prime Minister Nawaz Sharif,[97] speak of the goal of 'full spectrum deterrence' against the full spectrum of perceived Indian threats at the tactical, operational and strategic levels. Deterrence at the tactical level is defined as against limited incursions by Indian mechanised/armoured brigades and infantry divisions. At the operational level, deterrence refers to a sizeable military offensive including mechanised/armoured divisions, strike corps and corps-plus size forces. At the strategic level, it means preventing an all-out war involving two or more strike corps. Sultan adds that while the 60km-range *Nasr* can be considered a battlefield (tactical-use) weapon, the 180km-range *Abdali* provides an operational-level capability,[98] meaning it is for in-theatre use.

The purpose of introducing these shorter-range systems is to restore Pakistan's nuclear deterrence at lower rungs of crisis situations by denying India the space to operate below Pakistan's perceived nuclear threshold – in other words, 'to plug the deterrence gap'.[99] 'Full spectrum deterrence', which has come to supplant 'credible minimum deterrence' as the SPD's preferred catchphrase, means a menu of options from which to choose a proportionate response. Explaining the evolution, Sultan says moving toward 'full-spectrum' increases credibility. He thus employs the phrase 'a strategy of assured deterrence'.[100]

There is a contradiction between lowering the nuclear threshold by positing a flexible nuclear response and insisting, as is usually claimed, that the nuclear weapons would be used only as a last resort, 'in extremis conditions'.[101] The only answer is to redefine 'last resort'. Such redefining, however, can fuel apprehensions about a nation's true intent. Tertrais suggests, for example, that as Pakistan's arsenal and nuclear options grow, its doctrine could evolve toward not just flexible response, but escalation dominance.

No intention to operationalise *Nasr*

The irony about introducing tactical nuclear weapons is that they have little military utility in the role for which they are envisioned: stopping enemy tank offensives. As conclusively demonstrated by Pakistan-born physicists Abdul Hameed Nayyar and Zia Mian, the enemy can effectively diminish the impact by increasing the spacing between tanks. To stop half of a well-dispersed attacking force of 1,000 tanks would require 100 15kt weapons, nearly exhausting Pakistan's nuclear arsenal and making poor use of limited plutonium stockpiles.[102] Exponentially more weapons would be needed to stop enemy tank formations if the short-range nuclear weapons were sub-kiloton, as has been hinted.

It took some years for Pakistan to make up its mind on whether the smaller-yield weapons or indeed any of its weapons would have a war-fighting purpose. Of late, the planners have sought to emphasise that their role is purely for deterrence. Thus, when presented with calculations on the large number of low-yield weapons that would be needed to stop Indian tank formations, the SPD's answer is that only a few such nuclear weapons need be used for demonstration purposes, in order to initiate political moves to end the incursion.[103]

Pakistani military officials even suggest the counter-intuitive point that there is no plan to operationalise *Nasr*. On the basis of a final briefing by SPD before publication of his book in 2012, Feroz Khan wrote: 'Pakistan has no plans to move toward battlefield weapons.'[104] That is to say, there has been no decision to produce the weapon systems or to incorporate them into battlefield tactics or military doctrine. Ahmed adds a practical spin in making the same point: 'Pakistan will never have the fissile material production capacity to develop battlefield nuclear weapons for war-fighting even on a modest scale. Its existing stocks are only good enough for a few weapons for battlefield use mainly for deterrence purposes.'[105] Academic Christopher Clary, who handled South Asia nuclear issues while working in the Office of the US Secretary of Defense, calls the battlefield nuclear capability a 'force in being'.[106]

Monetary costs

As in most nuclear-armed states, the cost of Pakistan's nuclear weapons cannot be accurately measured because of the secrecy of most aspects of the programme. In 2001, retired Major-General Mahmud Ali Durrani estimated that for the next ten years, the programme would likely require about 0.5% of GDP per year.[107] This meant about US$2.5 billion in 2011, based on purchasing power parity (PPP) estimates of Pakistan's GDP, or about 10% of Pakistan's estimated conventional military budget in PPP terms.[108] In 2009, a Pakistani investigative journalist reached a similar conclusion about the relative size of nuclear spending.[109] It is about one-third of what India spends on its nuclear-weapons programme, which in 2010–11 was estimated to be US$7.7bn based on PPP.[110]

To these past calculations one must add the additional cost of the new plutonium-production reactors and reprocessing facilities, the expansion in size and complexity of the arsenal and the development of new delivery platforms. In Pakistan, however, the cost of the nuclear expansion is rarely questioned. Notwithstanding Pakistan's dismal economic state, the nuclear weapons are viewed by most citizens as a source of technological pride and as a necessity to protect national sovereignty. As Krepon puts it, 'money spent on the bomb' is not begrudged.[111] Recognising resource constraints, military leaders insist that they need to avoid a costly nuclear arms race with India. But they point to the huge disparity in overall military spending – Pakistan's military budget is only around 15% of India's[112] – and see nuclear weapons as a cost-effective equaliser.

Civilian nuclear sector

Pakistan's civilian nuclear sector is also under expansion. Three power reactors are currently in operation. In addition to the Canadian-supplied 137MWe KANUPP-1, which has been running for over 40 years, Pakistan has two 300MWe Chinese-built reactors at Chashma: CHASNUPP-1 (which went online in 2000) and CHASNUPP-2 (online in 2011). According to the IAEA, the three reactors contributed 5.34% of total energy output for 2012 (5,271.41 gigawatt hours (GWh) out of a total 98,709.60 GWh).[113] Hoodbhoy says the actual amount of electricity produced is around 1.6–1.8% of the total.[114] In either case, the contribution from nuclear power is small.

Two new 340MWe Chinese reactors under construction at Chashma are scheduled to begin commercial operation in 2016 and 2017. Under NSG guidelines, as a non-signatory to the NPT and lacking the exemption granted to India in 2008, Pakistan is ineligible for cooperation in nuclear energy. China claims that CHASNUPP-3 and -4 were exempted from NSG rules under a grandfather clause, on grounds that the reactors fall under the terms of a civil nuclear agreement struck with Pakistan in 1991 before China joined the NPT in 1992 and the NSG in 2004. Although China never provided details of the terms of the grandfathered deal, other NSG members acquiesced with varying degrees of enthusiasm.[115]

A deal for two more Chinese reactors – at 1,000MWe, three times larger than the others – was finalised in 2013. The new reactors are being built in Karachi, which complicates the grandfathering argument because the 1991 agreement was for power plants at Chashma.

The new China deal will be a first step toward fulfilment of PAEC's plans for a dramatic expansion of the nation's nuclear-energy infrastructure. In 2005 it was announced that the government had tasked the PAEC with the construction of 13 new civilian reactors to increase total capacity to 8,800MWe by 2030 to help solve the nation's energy crisis.[116] In the years since, the energy crisis has steadily worsened, becoming a major issue in the May 2013 elections that returned Nawaz

Sharif as prime minister. Lights often go out for at least ten hours a day in major cities and for up to 22 hours a day in rural areas, sparking deadly riots and denying 2–4 percentage points to annual GNP growth. The supply deficit is estimated to be around 3,000MWe.[117] At a groundbreaking ceremony for the new nuclear power plant at Karachi, Sharif announced a new plan – 'Nuclear Energy Vision 2050' – which envisages nuclear power generation of about 40,000MW by 2050.[118]

However, a shortage of generational capacity is not Pakistan's biggest energy problem. Distribution losses are staggering. The causes lie in corruption, mismanagement, pilfering and a chronic failure across all sectors of the economy to pay for energy consumed. These practices have produced a circular debt crisis that creates cash-flow problems through-out the energy supply chain, resulting in lack of maintenance and repairs and inability to import fuel oil.[119] According to Hoodbhoy: 'The solution lies in rigidly enforcing the rule: you use, you pay ... Stopping power theft would save far more megawatts than will be generated by Chashma's four nuclear reactors combined.'[120]

This is not to deny Pakistan's need to expand power genera-tional capacity to keep pace with the demand. But expanding the civilian nuclear infrastructure may not be the best solu-tion to the energy crisis, given the security implications, safety concerns in a country prone to earthquakes and floods, huge costs and long lead times. As US nuclear-energy analyst Toby Dalton has argued, 'with a highly unstable grid and moribund economy, there are cheaper and faster ways for Pakistan to improve its energy situation than using nuclear.'[121] He argues that improving efficiency by rehabilitating electricity trans-mission and distribution systems, rebuilding old turbines at hydroelectric facilities and incorporating combined cycle systems (the exhaust of one heat engine is used as the heat source for another) into new thermal electric generation facilities are three ways in which Pakistan could increase available electricity in the near term.[122] Renewable energy sources that, unlike nuclear, do not require a centralised power-generation source may also offer more promise for increasing electrification rates. Pakistan's solar energy potential is rivalled only by the Sahara[123] and there is significant potential for wind-power generation in the Gharo–Keti Bandar wind corridor.[124]

Notes

[1] The size of research reactors is generally measured in terms of thermal output, or 't', in contrast to electrical output, designated as 'e', for power reactors.

[2] Feroz H. Khan, *Eating Grass: The Making of the Pakistani Bomb* (Stanford, CA: Stanford University Press, 2012), pp. 60–61; Joseph Cirincione, Jon B. Wolfsthal and Miriam Rajkumar, *Deadly Arsenals: Nuclear, Biological and Chemical Threats* (Washington DC: Carnegie Endowment for International Peace, 2005), pp. 240–41.

[3] Cited in Kausar Niazi, *Zulfiqar Ali Bhutto of Pakistan, last days* (New Delhi: Vikas, 1992), p. 99. The quote is rendered with slight differences in various sources, usually with the operative phrase 'eat grass'.

[4] Zulfiqar Ali Bhutto, *The Myth of Independence* (Oxford: Oxford University Press, 1969), http://bhutto.org/Acrobat/Myth%20of%20Independence.pdf.

[5] Munir Ahmad Khan, Chagai Medal Award Ceremony Speech, 20 March 1999, PINSTECH Auditorium, Islamabad, http://www.nuclearfiles.org/menu/key-issues/

nuclear-weapons/issues/policy/pakistani-nuclear-policy/munir%20ahmad%20khan's%20speech.html.

[6] IISS, *Nuclear Black Markets: Pakistan, A.Q. Khan and the rise of proliferation networks – A net assessment* (London: IISS, 2007), p. 16.

[7] Today it is called the Institute of Industrial Control Systems.

[8] Promotional video of Khan Research Laboratories, quoted in Steve Coll, 'Atomic Emporium', *New Yorker*, 7 and 14 August 2006, p. 5.

[9] Khan, *Eating Grass*, pp. 153, 160.

[10] Ibid., pp. 184–85.

[11] Jeffrey T. Richelson, *Spying on the Bomb: American Nuclear Intelligence from Nazi Germany to Iran and North Korea* (New York: W.W. Norton & Co., 2006), p. 344.

[12] Khan, *Eating Grass*, p. 279.

[13] Ibid., pp. 281–82; and Samar Mubarakmand quoted in Shahid-ur-Rehman, *Long Road to Chagai* (Islamabad: Print Wise Publications, 1999), pp. 14–15.

[14] Richelson, *Spying on the Bomb*, p. 440.

[15] The theoretical possibilities include diversion of spent fuel from the Canadian-supplied KUNAPP-1

reactor before the IAEA was allowed to apply safeguards, with reprocessing at a pilot plant or via limited operations at the reprocessing facility that was then still under construction called New Labs. It is generally believed, however, that reprocessing was not yet possible.

16 Zia Mian et al., 'Fissile Materials in South Asia: The Implications of the U.S.-India Nuclear Deal', research report of the International Panel on Fissile Materials (IPFM), September 2006, p. 15, http://www.fissile materials.org/library/southasia.pdf.

17 Hans M. Kristensen and Robert S. Norris, 'Pakistan's nuclear forces, 2011', Bulletin of the Atomic Scientists, vol. 67, no. 4, July/August 2011, p. 93, http://bos.sagepub.com/content/67/4/91.full.pdf+html.

18 Robert S. Norris and Hans M. Kristensen, 'Nuclear Notebook: Pakistan's Nuclear Forces, 2007', Bulletin of the Atomic Scientists, vol. 63, no. 3, May/June 2007, pp. 71–73. The IAEA uses 25kg of 90% HEU as a benchmark 'significant quantity', defined as 'the approximate amount of nuclear material for which the possibility of manufacturing a nuclear explosive device cannot be excluded'. Weapons can be made with smaller amounts of HEU, however, and most experts believe that Pakistan uses 15–20kg.

19 Mark Hibbs, 'Pakistan Developed More Powerful Centrifuges', Nuclear Fuel, 29 January 2007. Centrifuge output is measured in separative work units (SWU). The P-2 model has a design capacity of five SWU per year, while the P-3 is estimated to produce just under ten

SWU per year and the P-4 about 20 SWU per year.

20 Pervez Hoodbhoy, 'Pakistan: Understanding the "World's Fastest Growing Arsenal"', in Pervez Hoodbhoy (ed.), Confronting the Bomb: Pakistani and Indian Scientists Speak Out (Karachi: Oxford University Press, 2013), p. 98.

21 In 1998, the US Department of Commerce listed 'ultracentrifuge' facilities at Golra and Sihala, and an 'enrichment plant' at Gadwal as subject to export restrictions. US Department of Commerce, Bureau of Export Administration, Federal Register, vol. 63, no. 223, 19 November 1998, http://www.gpo.gov/fdsys/pkg/FR-1998-11-19/pdf/98-30877.pdf.

22 David Albright, Paul Brannan and Robert Kelley, 'Pakistan Expanding Dera Ghazi Khan Site: Time for US to Call for Limits', 19 May 2009, http://isis-online.org/uploads/isis-reports/documents/PakistanExpanding CPC_19May2009.pdf.

23 Mansoor Ahmed, comment in Arms Control Wonk, 24 April 2013, http://krepon.armscontrolwonk.com/archive/3754/the-tortoise-and-the-hare-a-rebuttal.

24 Mansoor Ahmed, quoted in Michael Krepon, 'The Tortoise and the Hare: A Rebuttal', Arms Control Wonk, 23 April 2013, http://krepon.armscontrolwonk.com/archive/3754/the-tortoise-and-the-hare-a-rebuttal.

25 IPFM, Global Fissile Material Report 2010: Balancing the Books: Production and Stocks (Princeton, NJ: IPFM, 2010), p. 130.

26 IPFM, 'Countries: Pakistan', 3 February 2013, http://fissilematerials.org/countries/pakistan.html.

27 *Ibid.*

28 David Albright and Paul Brannan, 'Pakistan Appears to be Building a Third Plutonium Production Reactor at Khushab Nuclear Site', 21 June 2007, http://isis-online.org/uploads/isis-reports/documents/ThirdKhushabReactor.pdf.

29 Under the IAEA benchmark, 8kg of plutonium constitute a significant quantity, but most experts assess that Pakistan can produce bombs using less plutonium.

30 IPFM, 'Countries: Pakistan'.

31 Serena Kelleher-Vergantini and Robert Avagyan, 'Further Construction Progress on the Fourth Heavy Water Reactor at Khushab Nuclear Site', ISIS Imagery Brief, 20 December 2013, http://isis-online.org/uploads/isis-reports/documents/Khushab_November_2013.pdf.

32 Tamara Patton, 'Combining Satellite Imagery and 3D Drawing Tools for Nonproliferation Analysis: A Case Study of Pakistan's Khushab Plutonium Production Reactors', *Science & Global Security*, vol. 20, nos. 2–3, 2012, pp. 117–40, http://scienceandglobalsecurity.org/archive/2012/10/combining_satellite_imagery_an.html.

33 Unconfirmed and unattributed information from Pakistani sources suggests that Khushab-2 and -3 are identical in size to Khushab-1. Communication with Pakistani scholar, November 2013.

34 Institute for Science and International Security, 'New Satellite Image of Chashma Nuclear Site in Pakistan', 9 July 2010, http://isis-online.org/isis-reports/detail/new-satellite-image-of-chashma-nuclear-site-in-pakistan/.

35 David Albright and Paul Brannan, 'Pakistan Expanding Plutonium Separation Facility Near Rawalpindi', 19 May 2009, http://www.isis-online.org/publications/southasia/PakistanExpandingNewlabs.pdf.

36 Catherine Collins and Douglas Frantz, *Fallout: The True Story of the CIA's Secret War on Nuclear Trafficking* (New York: Free Press, 2011), pp. 195, 201, 204.

37 Thomas C. Reed and Danny B. Stillman, *The Nuclear Express: A Political History of the Bomb and Its Proliferation* (Minneapolis, MN: Zenith Press, 2009), p. 52.

38 Briefing by Peter Lavoy, US National Intelligence Officer for South Asia, to NATO Permanent Representatives, 25 November 2008, summarised in classified US cable, 5 December 2008, http://www.cablegatesearch.net/cable.php?id=08USNATO453&version=1315488573.

39 Robert S. Norris and Hans M. Kristensen, 'Global nuclear weapons inventories, 1945–2010', *Bulletin of the Atomic Scientists*, July 2010, vol. 66, no. 4, pp. 77–83; Zia Mian, 'Pakistan', in Ray Acheson (ed.), *Assuring Destruction Forever: Nuclear Weapon Modernization Around the World* (New York: Reaching Critical Will of the Women's International League for Peace and Freedom, 2012), p. 51, http://www.reachingcriticalwill.org/images/documents/Publications/modernization/assuring-destruction-forever.pdf.

40 David Sanger and Eric Schmitt, 'Pakistani Nuclear Arms Pose Challenge to U.S. Policy', *New York Times*, 31 January 2011.

41 *Ibid.*

42 David Albright, 'Pakistan Doubling Rate of Making Nuclear Weapons: Time for Pakistan to Reverse Course', ISIS Reports, 16 May 2011, http://isis-online.org/uploads/isis-reports/documents/Fourth_Khushab_Military_Reactor_16May2011_1.pdf.

43 Kristensen and Norris, 'Pakistan's nuclear forces, 2011'.

44 Hoodbhoy, 'Pakistan', p. 100.

45 Thomas B. Cochran, 'What is the Size of Khushab II?', Natural Resources Defense Council, 8 September 2006, p. 18, http://docs.nrdc.org/nuclear/files/nuc_06090801A.pdf.

46 Hoodbhoy, 'Pakistan', p. 101.

47 Zia Mian, A.H. Nayyar and R. Rajaraman, 'Exploring Uranium Resource Constraints on Fissile Material Production in Pakistan', *Science and Global Security*, vol. 17, nos. 2–3, 2009, p. 84, http://www.princeton.edu/sgs/publications/sgs/archive/17-2-3-Mian-Nay-Raj.pdf.

48 Mansoor Ahmed, comment in Arms Control Wonk, 23 April 2013, http://krepon.armscontrolwonk.com/archive/3754/the-tortoise-and-the-hare-a-rebuttal.

49 Tamara Patton, 'Patton on Pakistan's U Supply', Arms Control Wonk, 3 December 2012, http://lewis.armscontrolwonk.com/archive/5928/patton-on-pakistans-u-supply.

50 Statement by Ambassador Zamir Akram at the Conference of Disarmament, 18 February 2010. A decade earlier, Zamir Akram's brother Munir, similarly in the position of ambassador to the Conference on Disarmament, said India had enough fissile material to produce over 400 nuclear weapons. See 'Indian Nuclear Doctrine', Statement by Ambassador Munir Akram at the Conference on Disarmament, 19 August 1999, http://www.fas.org/news/pakistan/1999/CD-20August99.htm.

51 Vivek Raghuvanshi, 'India to Stay the Course on Nuke Doctrine', *Defense News*, 1 November 2004.

52 Michael Krepon, 'Pakistan's Nuclear Strategy and Deterrence Stability', Stimson Center, 10 December 2012, http://www.stimson.org/images/uploads/research-pdfs/Krepon_-_Pakistan_Nuclear_Strategy_and_Deterrence_Stability.pdf.

53 Discussions in Rawalpindi and Islamabad, November 2011 and December 2013.

54 Author interview, March 2013.

55 Author interview, June 2013.

56 *Hatf*, meaning vengeance or sword of Muhammad in Urdu, is the class name assigned to all of Pakistan's ballistic missiles.

57 Bruno Tertrais, 'Pakistan's nuclear programme: a net assessment', Fondation pour la Recherche Stratégique, 13 June 2012, p. 12, http://www.frstrategie.org/barreFRS/publications/rd/2012/RD_201204.pdf.

58 Usman Ansari, 'Pakistan Tests "Nuke-Capable" Short-Range Missile', *Defense News*, 20 April 2011.

59 Rajaram Nagappa, Arun Vishwanathan and Aditi Malhotra, 'HATF-IX/NASR – Pakistan's Tactical Nuclear Weapon: Implications for Indo-Pak Deterrence', National Institute of Advanced Studies, Bangalore, India, July 2013, http://isssp.in/

wp-content/uploads/2013/07/R17-2013_NASR_Final.pdf. Several other sources assume the diameter to be 300mm, apparently because this is the calibre of the rockets used by the Chinese A-100 TEL that Pakistan imported as the chassis for the *Nasr*. The difference is significant. The United States has developed 11 missile nuclear warheads with a diameter less than 350mm, but most would not fit a missile with a diameter of 300mm.

60 Zahir Kazmi, 'SRBMs, Deterrence and Regional Stability in South Asia: A Case Study of Nasr and Prahaar', Institute of Regional Studies, 2012, p. 46, http://www.irs.org.pk/strategic/sps012.pdf.

61 Martin Sieff, 'Pakistan Tests Hatf Again', UPI, 21 February 2006, http://www.spacewar.com/reports/Pakistan_Tests_Hatf_Again.html.

62 Inter Services Public Relations (ISPR), Press Release, 5 March 2012, http://www.ispr.gov.pk/front/main.asp?o=t-press_release&date=2012/3/5.

63 ISPR, Press Release, 17 September 2012, http://www.ispr.gov.pk/front/main.asp?o=t-press_release&date=2012/9/17; and 'Nuclear-capable cruise missile test-fired from Mirage fighter', *Dawn*, 29 April 2011, http://dawn.com/2011/04/30/nuclear-capable-cruise-missile-test-fired-from-mirage-fighter/.

64 'Hatf-7, Babur Cruise Missile', Pakistani military blog, 31 August 2012, http://thatspakistan.blogspot.co.uk/2012/08/hatf-7-babur-cruise-missile.html.

65 ISPR, 'Naval Chief Inaugurates Naval Strategic Force Head-quarters', 19 May 2012, http://www.ispr.gov.pk/front/main.asp?o=t-press_release&id=2067.

66 Farhan Bokhari, 'Pakistan to Start Formal Talks with China to Buy Submarines', *Jane's Defence Weekly*, 18 March 2011.

67 Usman Ansari, 'Experts Wary of Pakistan Nuke Claims', *Defense News*, 26 May 2012, http://www.defensenews.com/article/20120526/DEFREG03/305260001/.

68 Jeffrey Lewis, 'Pakistan's Nuclear Artillery?', Arms Control Wonk, 12 December 2011, http://lewis.armscontrolwonk.com/archive/4866/pakistans-nuclear-artillery. Some experts believe, however, that sufficiently miniaturised warheads can be made with HEU. See Kapil Kak, 'Rationale and Implications', in Gurmeet Kanwal and Monika Chansoria, *Pakistan's Tactical Nuclear Weapons; Conflict Redux* (New Delhi: KW Publishers, 2014), pp. 70–71.

69 Mansoor Ahmed, presentation at EU Non-proliferation and Disarmament Conference, 1 October 2013, https://www.iiss.org/en/events/eu%20conference/sections/eu-conference-2013-ca57/special-sessions-3818/special-session-10-f279. See also Kazmi, 'SRBMs, Deterrence and Regional Stability in South Asia', pp. 5–6.

70 See, for example, Nagappa, Vishwanathan and Malhotra, 'HATF-IX/NASR – Pakistan's Tactical Nuclear Weapon'.

71 Feroz Khan, 'Prospects for Indian and Pakistani Arms Control', in Henry Sokolski (ed.), *The Next Arms Race* (Carlisle, PA: Strategic Studies Institute, 2012), p. 369, http://

www.npolicy.org/userfiles/image/ub1113.pdf.

72 Krepon, 'Pakistan's Nuclear Strategy and Deterrence Stability', p. 7.

73 'IISS Nuclear Doctrines Workshops in India and Pakistan', IISS Newsletter, Spring 2013, p. 11, http://www.iiss.org/-/media/Silos/Newsletters/2013/Spring-Newsletter-2013/IISS-Newsletter-Spring-2013.pdf.

74 Krepon, 'Pakistan's Nuclear Strategy and Deterrence Stability', p. 8.

75 Ibid.; and Agha Shahi, Zulfiqar Ali Khan and Abdul Sattar, 'Securing Nuclear Peace', News International, 5 October 1999.

76 Paul Kerr, 'U.S. Nuclear Cooperation with India: Issues for Congress', Congressional Research Service, 26 June 2012, p. 13, http://www.fas.org/sgp/crs/nuke/RL33016.pdf.

77 Abdul Sattar, address to the 'Pakistan Response to the Indian Nuclear Doctrine' Seminar, 25 November 1999; available in Disarmament Diplomacy, no. 41, November 1999.

78 Khan, Eating Grass, pp. 372–73.

79 'Musharraf vows to "unleash a storm" if India attacks', News International, 30 May 2002.

80 Quoted in Siddharth Srivastava, 'War and peace, Musharraf-style', Asia Times, 24 May 2005, http://www.atimes.com/atimes/South_Asia/GC24Df03.html.

81 Tertrais, 'Pakistan's nuclear programme', p. 6.

82 ISPR, Press Release, 14 December 2010, www.ispr.gov.pk/front/main.asp?o=t-press_release&date=2010/12/14.

83 A 24 April 2013 speech by former foreign secretary Shyam Saran on India's nuclear posture, for example, repeatedly emphasised the need for credibility and never stated it to be minimal. 'Is India's Nuclear Deterrent Credible?', speech by Shyam Saran, New Delhi, 24 April 2013, http://southasiamonitor.org/detail.php?type=pers&nid=4987.

84 IISS discussions in Islamabad, March 2013.

85 A 22 November 2008 unscripted remark by newly appointed President Asif Ali Zandari that Pakistan would not use nuclear weapons first was not subsequently repeated. Jawed Naqvi, 'Zardari suggests accord to avoid nuclear conflict in S. Asia', Dawn, 23 November 2008.

86 'IISS Nuclear Doctrines Workshops in India and Pakistan'.

87 'Press Conference by New Permanent Representative of Pakistan', UN Press Briefing, 29 May 2002, http://www.un.org/News/briefings/docs/2002/pakistanpc.doc.htm.

88 Krepon, 'Pakistan's Nuclear Strategy and Deterrence Stability', p. 10.

89 Tertrais, 'Pakistan's nuclear programme', p. 7.

90 Paolo Cotta-Ramusino and Maurizio Martellini, 'Nuclear Safety, Nuclear Stability and Nuclear Strategy in Pakistan: A Concise Report of a Visit by Landau Network–Centro Volta', 14 January 2002, http://www.pugwash.org/september11/pakistan-nuclear.htm.

91 Christopher Clary, 'Thinking about Pakistan's Nuclear Security in Peacetime, Crisis and War', Institute

for Defence Studies and Analyses, Occasional Paper No. 12, September 2010, p. 26; Tertrais, 'Pakistan's nuclear programme', p. 8.

92 Krepon, 'Pakistan's Nuclear Strategy and Deterrence Stability', pp. 11–12.

93 Peter Lavoy, 'Islamabad's Nuclear Posture: Its Premises and Implementation', in Henry Sokolski (ed.), *Pakistan's Nuclear Future: Worries Beyond War* (Carlisle, PA: Strategic Studies Institute, 2008), p. 158. See also Kerr, 'U.S. Nuclear Cooperation with India', p. 9.

94 Kerr, 'U.S. Nuclear Cooperation with India', p. 13.

95 Quoted in Sumit Ganguly and S. Paul Kapur, *India, Pakistan, and the Bomb: Debating Nuclear Stability in South Asia* (New York: Columbia University Press, 2007), pp. 77–78.

96 Adil Sultan, 'South Asian Stability-Instability Paradox: An Alternate Perspective', unpublished paper, 2013, p. 15.

97 Nawaz Sharif, 'Nuclear bombs provide deterrence against external aggression', *Economic Times of India*, 19 June 2013.

98 Adil Sultan, 'Pakistan's emerging nuclear posture: impact of drivers and technology on nuclear doctrine', Institute of Strategic Studies Islamabad, 17 April 2012, p. 162, http://www.issi.org.pk/publication-files/1340000409_86108059.pdf.

99 *Ibid.*, pp. 159, 162.

100 *Ibid.*, pp. 160–61.

101 See, for example, Zafar Khan, 'Pakistan's policy of arms control and disarmament: a call for an arms control regime in South Asia', *Defence Studies*, vol. 13, no. 1, 2013, p. 69.

102 A.H. Nayyar and Zia Mian, 'The Limited Military Utility of Pakistan's Battlefield Use of Nuclear Weapons in Response to Large Scale Indian Conventional Attack', Pakistan Security Research Unit, Brief Number 61, 11 November 2010, p. 7, http://www.princeton.edu/sgs/faculty-staff/zia-mian/Limited-Military-Utility-of-Pakistans.pdf.

103 Sultan, 'Pakistan's emerging nuclear posture', p.160.

104 Khan, *Eating Grass*, p. 396.

105 Mansoor Ahmed's rebuttal, cited in Krepon, 'The Tortoise and the Hare', Arms Control Wonk, 23 April 2013.

106 Christopher Clary, 'Pakistan: The Future of Pakistan's Nuclear Weapons Program', in Ashley J. Tellis, Abraham M. Denmark and Travis Tanner, *Strategic Asia 2013-2014: Asia in the Second Nuclear Age* (Seattle, WA: National Bureau of Asian Research, 2013), p. 132.

107 Mahmud Ali Durrani, *India and Pakistan: The Cost of Conflict and the Benefits of Peace* (Karachi: Oxford University Press, 2001), p. 32.

108 Mian, 'Pakistan', in Acheson (ed.), *Assuring Destruction Forever*, p. 55.

109 Ansar Abbasi, 'Pak Nuclear Programme Faces 35 pc Cut', *News International*, 1 May 2009.

110 Bruce G. Blair and Matthew A. Brown, 'World Spending on Nuclear Weapons Surpasses $1 Trillion per Decade', Global Zero Technical Report, June 2011, http://www.globalzero.org/files/gz_nuclear_weapons_cost_study.pdf.

111 Krepon, 'Pakistan's Nuclear Strategy and Deterrence Stability', p. 6.

112 According to the IISS *Military Balance*, India's military spending

in 2013 was $US36.3bn compared to Pakistan's $US5.89bn. IISS, *The Military Balance 2014* (Abingdon: Routledge for IISS, 2014).

[113] IAEA, Power Reactor Information System, Pakistan, 2013, http://www.iaea.org/PRIS/CountryStatistics/CountryDetails.aspx?current=PK.

[114] Pervez Hoodbhoy, 'Nuclear electricity for Pakistan is not the answer', in Hoodbhoy (ed.), *Confronting the Bomb*, p. 328.

[115] The 1991 agreement and subsequent contract between CNNC and PAEC were understood to be specific to Chashma. An earlier 1986 civilian nuclear-cooperation agreement between China and Pakistan was generic. See Mark Hibbs, 'The Future of the Nuclear Suppliers Group', Carnegie Endowment for International Peace, 2011, p. 14, http://carnegieendowment.org/files/future_nsg.pdf.

[116] Ihtasham ul Haque, 'PAEC told to set up 13 N-power plants', *Dawn*, 15 July 2005.

[117] 'Mounting circular debt to worsen power crisis', *Nation*, 11 April 2013; 'PM orders inquiry into power theft, defaults to oil suppliers', *Pakistan Today*, 6 April 2013; Kaswar Klasra, 'Rs90b lost in power theft, Senate told', *Nation*, 9 March 2013; and Toby Dalton et al., 'A Criteria-Based Approach to Nuclear Cooperation With Pakistan', Carnegie Policy Outlook, 22 June 2011, http://carnegieendowment.org/files/nsg_criteria.pdf.

[118] 'PM speech at Karachi Coastal Power Project (K-2/K-3) Ground Breaking Ceremony', Prime Minister's Office, Islamic Republic of Pakistan, 26 November 2013, http://www.pmo.gov.pk/pm_speech_details.php?speech_id=20.

[119] Amin Ahmed, 'PC blames govt for circular debt crisis', *Dawn*, 27 March 2012, http://dawn.com/2013/03/27/pc-blames-govt-for-circular-debt-crisis/; and 'The Causes and Impacts of Power Sector Circular Debt in Pakistan', USAID, March 2013, p. 7, http://www.pc.gov.pk/hot%20links/2013/Final_USAID-Pakistan%20Circular%20Debt%20Report-Printed%20Mar%2025,%202013.pdf.

[120] Hoodbhoy, 'Nuclear electricity for Pakistan is not the answer', p. 342.

[121] Tom Hundley, 'Did Pakistan Join the Wrong Nuclear Club?', Pulitzer Center, 11 July 2012, http://pulitzercenter.org/reporting/pakistan-india-nuclear-arms-race-energy-reactors.

[122] Toby Dalton, 'The Myth of Nuclear Energy in Pakistan', *Foreign Policy*, 17 May 2011, http://afpak.foreignpolicy.com/posts/2011/05/17/the_myth_of_nuclear_energy_in_pakistan. See also John Stephenson and Peter Tynan, 'Is Nuclear Power Pakistan's Best Energy Investment? Assessing Pakistan's Electricity Situation', in Sokolski (ed.), *Pakistan's Nuclear Future*, pp. 103–30, http://www.npolicy.org/userfiles/image/s%20Electricity%20Situation_pdf.pdf.

[123] Angelika Wasielke (ed.), 'Energy-policy Framework Conditions for Electricity Markets and Renewable Energies: 23 Country Analyses', GTZ, Eschborn, September 2007, p. 11, http://www.giz.de/expertise/downloads/Fachexpertise/giz2007-en-windenergy-countrystudy.pdf.

pdf; and Stephenson and Tynan, 'Is Nuclear Power Pakistan's Best Energy Investment?', p. 110.

124 Khurram Baig, 'Energy mix: Despite multiple options, Pakistan should not give up on hydel', *Express Tribune*, 30 June 2013, http://tribune.com.pk/story/570486/energy-mix-despite-multiple-options-pakistan-should-not-give-up-on-hydel/.

CHAPTER TWO

The potential for nuclear use

If the global taboo on nuclear use that has prevailed since 1945 is ever broken, a common view among foreign-policy commentators is that it will happen in South Asia.[1] It would be an exaggeration to call the subcontinent a nuclear tinderbox. Despite occasional border incidents, the chances of a nuclear exchange seem low. Yet India and Pakistan have gone to war three times in the last seven decades, and nearly come to blows several other times. The source of greatest contention – the territorial dispute over Kashmir – remains unresolved. With that dispute in the background, the potential for a triggering incident via a cross-border terrorist atrocity remains ever possible. Given India's stated deterrence policy and the nuclear-response doctrines enunciated by both sides, it is not hard to imagine a conventional conflict escalating to nuclear use. US President Bill Clinton in 2000 famously referred to South Asia as 'the most dangerous place in the world'.[2] US non-proliferation expert George Perkovich more recently explained why: 'Never have nuclear competitors been in an environment like India–Pakistan, where there is a seamless spectrum from sub-conventional to strategic.'[3]

Most strategists in South Asia contend that their nuclear weapons serve to keep conflicts from escalating, in a regional version of the Cold War-origin concept of 'Mutual Assured Destruction' (MAD). Kenneth Waltz's theory of nuclear weapons as a stabilising force[4] may well hold true in South Asia. Since each became an overt nuclear power in 1998 by testing nuclear weapons, the several conflicts that have broken out have been kept to low levels of intensity. Each side knows that escalation could bring a devastating response.

Yet even if the MAD equation works in the subcontinent, the possession of nuclear weapons has probably engendered a larger number of limited wars by encouraging risk taking. The subcontinent exemplifies the 'stability/instability' paradox of international-relations theory, which holds that when two adversaries each obtain nuclear weapons, the probability of a direct war between them greatly decreases, while the probability of minor or indirect conflicts increases. In 1999, for example, Chief of Army Staff Pervez Musharraf was emboldened to encroach on territory across the Line of Control (LoC) in northern Kashmir in the expectation that his nation's nuclear weapons would deter a forceful Indian counter-strike against Pakistani territory. Some scholars disagree that the 'stability/instability' paradox accounts for such crises or they suggest more complicated patterns of interaction,[5] but most contend that nuclear weapons in South Asia have indeed induced a greater propensity for adventurism.[6]

A propensity for low-level conflict is worrisome because of the prospect of nuclear-weapons use arising through accident or miscalculation. There is no reason to think that India and Pakistan are less careful with nuclear weapons than the superpowers have been. This is little reassurance, however, given the long history of nuclear mishaps and near misses involving the United States and the Soviet Union.[7] And the superpowers had more time to work out safety procedures to prevent accidents at home and transparency measures to prevent misperceptions abroad. India and Pakistan are still relative newcomers to the nuclear field and have too few reliable processes for preventing mishaps.

Accidents are one thing; mistakes are another. The most worrisome nuclear danger in South Asia is the deliberate use of nuclear weapons as a result of miscalculation and misperception. There is a grave concern that another large-scale cross-border terrorist incident in India on the scale of the 2001 parliament attack and the 2008 Mumbai atrocity would provoke a negative spiral that could lead to nuclear war. Several factors contribute to the growing risk.

The escalatory cycle begins with sub-conventional (terrorist) threats. The number of jihadists in Pakistan swelled after the US-led intervention in Afghanistan. The use of drone strikes against militant targets in Pakistan killed many militant leaders but resulted in more Pashtuns becoming radicalised.[8] A metastasising phenomenon has seen the number of terrorist groups expanding.[9] Qualitative increases in terrorist capabilities and violence levels, plus new interactions among terrorist groups act as force multipliers. With Pakistan's internal situation likely to remain dire for decades, another terrorist attack against India is widely seen as a matter of when, not if. As US forces leave Afghanistan, extremists may turn renewed attention to Kashmir, as was the case following the Soviet withdrawal from Afghanistan in the early 1990s, or to India proper.

India's response to the next terrorist attack may not be as restrained as in 2001 and 2008. As Perkovich aptly puts it, the 'neo-Gandhian forbearance' that India displayed in the former crises is unlikely to persist as new leaders emerge in New Delhi.[10] There is a strong sense in India today that deterrence credibility must be restored by responding forcefully to any further attack. As described in Chapter Three, Indian Army officials in 2004 unveiled a plan to allow their forces to mobilise quickly in response to a terrorist attack and carry out a limited incursion into Pakistani territory in retaliation. An element of that plan, called 'Cold Start', created negative repercussions on a scale that lends new meaning to the adage 'be careful what you wish for'.

Although Cold Start may be little more than an aspiration without government approval, Pakistan in response has developed a battlefield-use nuclear posture. Judging that India sought to exploit a gap in Pakistan's nuclear-deterrence posture, the Pakistani military announced a lowering of its nuclear-use threshold. Nuclear weapons would now be used not just in cases where Pakistan faced an existential threat, but also against limited conventional attacks. The redefining of non-existential threats as being existential could lead to a failure of deterrence in a crisis. India's own nuclear policy in turn calls for massive retaliation against any nuclear attack against the nation. The escalation pattern runs from sub-conventional attacks through to conventional war and limited nuclear use to countervalue nuclear exchanges targeting cities.

Ambiguous red lines for nuclear retaliation exacerbate the potential for miscalculation, and the development of dual-use systems in both countries increases the risk of misperception. The ambiguity of dual-use systems could make it impossible to discriminate between nuclear and conventional attacks in real time during conflict. The expansion of the arms race to cruise missiles, ballistic-missile defence, submarine platforms and multiple independently targetable re-entry vehicle (MIRV) capabilities could further contribute to crisis instability. Whereas South Asian military strategists to date have agreed that nuclear war could not succeed, new capabilities leading to new military logic could drive a faster escalation to nuclear war. Geographic proximity and the inefficiency of early-warning capabilities exacerbate the risk, especially if there is a move away from recessed deployment of nuclear weapons.

One key external development adds to the danger. In past India–Pakistan crises, the United States often played a significant crisis-management role. Pakistan tended to count on Washington for a 'deus ex machina' solution when misadventures got out of hand. India, while far less eager for outside intervention, usually accepted US diplomatic initiatives as a contribution to avoiding major war. In the future, Washington will be less able to play this role, due to its diminished influence as a result of alleged affronts to Pakistani sovereignty[11] and the coming withdrawal of US front-line forces from Afghanistan. In addition, New Delhi may be less willing to accept US mediation that is seen to undercut India's deterrence posture.

India–Pakistan conflicts in the nuclear age[12]

In assessing the stability/instability paradox in South Asia, it is useful to examine the five major crises since 1986, each of which had a nuclear dimension to some degree. As Pakistan's nuclear capabilities transitioned to de facto and then overt status, the risks associated with crisis escalation became alarmingly more profound. While nuclear possession may have kept the crises from escalating, in some of the situations it emboldened risk taking.

1986–87 *Brasstacks* crisis

The timeframe when Pakistan is thought to have crossed the nuclear-weapon threshold during the mid-1980s coincided with a period of renewed tensions on the subcontinent. The first incident occurred in 1984 when the Indian military launched an operation to secure the Siachen Glacier region, a contested, un-demarcated area to the northeast of Kashmir in the Himalaya Mountains beyond the LoC.[13] Both militaries now hold positions in this uninhabited glacier. In summer 1986, the Indian military began a long-term series of military exercises known as *Operation Brasstacks*, which involved manoeuvres in the northern desert state of Rajasthan, near the Pakistani province of Sindh. These war games were the largest massing of military forces in South Asia since the Second World War and similar in size to those conducted by NATO in Europe.

While *Brasstacks* followed the pattern of previous Indian military exercises, it was perceived with great alarm in Rawalpindi, headquarters of the Pakistani army. In addition to the size of the exercises and the use of live munitions, the manoeuvres were conducted amidst growing Indian concern over the progress of Pakistan's nuclear programme. Moreover, New Delhi believed that Pakistani support was contributing to increased insurgent violence in both Indian Kashmir and Punjab.[14]

As a result of the deteriorating situation in Kashmir, the Indian Mountain Division was deployed to the region. With the positioning of two Indian forces so close to the border and the LoC, Pakistan feared a two-pronged Indian attack. During the third stage of *Brasstacks* in late 1986, Rawalpindi began its own military exercises, which were common during the winter months. However, the Pakistani manoeuvres, which also took place close to the border, were perceived by New Delhi as provocative and triggered Indian defensive positioning.

The crisis reached its apogee in January 1987 with 340,000 troops deployed along the border/LoC and military-to-military communication severed by the deactivation of the hotline between the directors general of military operations. It appears that the Indian leadership realised the deployment could have been misperceived as preparation for war. Therefore, a few days before the deployment was completed, India announced the defensive nature of its military movements and privately communicated a willingness to negotiate a joint withdrawal. With the help of US diplomatic intermediaries, the crisis was defused by a staged withdrawal from the border.[15]

Some accounts have suggested that *Brasstacks* was a ruse to provoke a Pakistani response that, in turn, would justify an Indian assault on Pakistan's nuclear facilities.[16] However, most scholars agree that the goal of the operation was to determine the command-and-control effectiveness of new mechanised units, as well as to demonstrate India's military resolve.[17]

This crisis did not really have the potential for nuclear escalation. While some accounts have claimed that Pakistan had already crossed the nuclear-weapons threshold, it did not have a means of delivery. However, during this crisis Pakistan for the first time conveyed a willingness to resort to nuclear weapons. On 28 January 1987, A.Q. Khan confirmed Pakistan's nuclear capability during an interview with Indian journalist Kuldip Nayar.[18] While the interview was not published until six weeks later, Nayar is understood to have immediately passed on the implicit threat to the Indian High Commission.[19] Pakistani Foreign Affairs Minister Zain Noorani also relayed the veiled threat by telling his Indian counterpart that if any Indian action threatened Pakistan's sovereignty and territorial integrity, Pakistan was 'capable of inflicting unacceptable damage'.[20]

There were several other nuclear aspects to the *Brasstacks* crisis. According to some scholars, Pakistan's new nuclear capability emboldened the military to aid the Kashmir insurgency, in the belief that nuclear weapons neutralised India's conventional military advantages.[21] Also, it should be noted that before the nuclear threats issued by Khan and Noorani, India had itself issued a nuclear threat by mooting the possibility of military strikes against the Kahuta enrichment plant.[22] Within two years of the crisis, Pakistan and India formalised their first nuclear confidence-building measure (CBM): an agreement on the Prohibition of Attack against Nuclear Installations and Facilities. This CBM, which is still in effect today, requires each party at every new year to provide the other with a list of nuclear facilities and locations.

1990 Kashmir crisis

The de-escalation of the *Brasstacks* crisis did little to quell the unrest in Kashmir and Punjab. Pakistan continued its support of insurgents in both regions. The low-level insurgency in Kashmir was further inflamed by the growing discontent with the political status quo. By 1990, frustrations, which had been largely expressed through demonstrations and strikes, turned violent with daily clashes between insurgents and security forces. This caused New Delhi to dissolve the State Assembly and place the region under direct governor's rule, subsequently triggering a full-blown insurgency in the region.

Also confronting a continued Sikh insurgency in Punjab, India deployed additional military units to augment security forces in both regions to prevent militant infiltration from Pakistani territory. Pakistan responded by moving armoured units to Pakistani territories opposite the Indian advancements. Pakistani forces that participated in the December 1989 *Zarb-e-Momin* military exercises – the largest in Pakistan's history – remained in their exercise area near the city of Multan and the LoC in Kashmir, rather than returning to their peacetime stations. Tensions escalated further in February 1990 during India's winter military exercises when armoured units were moved to the Mahajan training range in Rajasthan, located 160km from Multan. By April, approximately 200,000 Indian troops were matched across the LoC in Kashmir by roughly 100,000 Pakistani soldiers, both armies had deployed infantry near the border in Punjab and three Indian divisions in

Rajasthan were opposed across the border by a Pakistani corps.

During the elevated tensions, both air forces were put on heightened states of alert. Various reports indicate that at this point Pakistan assembled its first nuclear weapon.[23] Citing unsubstantiated US intelligence reports, journalistic accounts went further, claiming Pakistani military convoys transported nuclear weapons from storage to a nearby airfield, where they were deployed on F-16s.[24] These claims are seemingly corroborated by Pakistani Chief of Army Staff General Mirza Aslam Beg, who later said that Bhutto 'ordered the army and air force to get ready. A squadron of F-16s were moved to Mauripur and we pulled out our devices ... to arm the aircraft.'[25] In order to trigger US intervention to restrain Indian escalation, Pakistan appeared intent on signalling to the United States that it was prepared to use its nuclear capabilities.[26]

If this was the intent, it worked. Washington became increasingly concerned as tensions mounted in the subcontinent. Richard Kerr, former CIA deputy director, described the stand-off as: 'The most dangerous nuclear situation we have ever faced since I've been in the U.S. government. It may be as close as we've come to a nuclear exchange. It was far more frightening than the Cuban missile crisis.'[27]

Despite the escalatory military deployments and aggressive political climate, there is little credible evidence in public sources to suggest that the crisis came close to nuclear war. Both sides had a covert nuclear capability, known to the other side.[28] Yet S.K. Singh, Indian foreign secretary during this period, commented that the idea that India and Pakistan were on the brink of war in 1990 was a 'fairy tale' and described the situation as 'an elephantine Non-Crisis'. During the stand-off neither side engaged in behaviour typically associated with conflict preparation – for example, dumping ammunition, laying mines, cancelling military leave or moving armoured units towards the border.[29]

Apprehension about war in both capitals is evident from the rapidity with which the situation was defused. Following Indian Defence Secretary Naresh Chandra's trip to Pakistan and the subsequent meeting of foreign ministers on the side-lines of the UN General Assembly in late April, the two sides refrained from further troop deployments and agreed to reduce tensions. In late May, US Deputy National Security Advisor Robert Gates arrived in the region and offered intelligence assistance to verify a mutual military withdrawal. Shortly after his departure, the crisis was over.

Some have posited that Pakistan's alleged nuclear assembly during the crisis was a deliberate signal to trigger US inter-vention and restrain further escalation by India.[30] However, according to Prime Minister Benazir Bhutto: 'In 1990 we had not put together the bomb … if we had considered (the crisis) a serious threat; we would have had a meeting of the nuclear command committee, and put together the device. We never did that.'[31] It is conceivable that Bhutto was not apprised of the Pakistani army's war preparations. If the military was prepared to resort to nuclear use, it remains unclear if it had the requi-site delivery capability at this time. According to one account, by 1990 the Pakistan Atomic Energy Commission (PAEC) and Pakistan Air Force (PAF) had developed and operation-alised a nuclear bomb capable of being delivered by fighter jet.[32] President Musharraf, however, said that as late as 1999 Pakistan's nuclear capability was still 'not yet operational'.[33]

1999 Kargil crisis

The nuclear tests by India and Pakistan in May 1998 perma-nently altered the security dynamic in South Asia. In an effort to mitigate the risks associated with this demonstration of their respective nuclear capabilities, the prime ministers of India and Pakistan in February 1999 signed the Lahore Declaration. This was the first major agreement between the two countries since the end of the 1971 war. The agreement reaffirmed the commitment to resolve the Kashmir issue peacefully and to discuss confidence-building measures, both nuclear and conventional, to prevent future conflict. This effort at rapprochement, however, was short lived.

During the winter of 1998–99, Pakistani paramilitary forces[34] crossed the LoC and took up several positions in the mountainous Kargil–Dras sector of Kashmir. Since the harsh winter weather typically required the withdrawal of troops from their forward positions, the incursion went unnoticed by India. The goal of the operation was twofold. Politically, the Pakistanis wanted to re-establish international focus on the Kashmir issue; militarily, they hoped to secure a vantage point over the Srinagar-Leh highway to cut India's only communication/supply line to the Siachen Glacier. It is believed that Pakistan's military began planning an incursion in Kargil in the late 1980s in response to India's 1984 operation that secured the glacier's strategic elevations.

By the time India was alerted to the infiltration in early May 1999, about 2,000 Pakistani forces had secured positions across a 150–200km segment of formerly Indian-controlled territory, 8–12km east of the LoC. New Delhi responded to the operation by deploying roughly 200,000 troops and 60 cargo aircraft to the Kargil sector to expel the Pakistani forces and re-establish the LoC. New Delhi split three strike corps between Punjab and Rajasthan and moved Indian naval forces into the Arabian Sea in preparations for an expanded conflict, but refrained from opening additional battlefronts. Rawalpindi responded to the Indian deployments with like preparations of its land, air and sea forces. Meanwhile, between 26 May and 30 June

Indian and Pakistani officials and leaders exchanged direct or indirect nuclear threats no fewer than 13 times, almost evenly divided.[35]

After nearly two months of conflict, Prime Minister Nawaz Sharif agreed to Pakistan's withdrawal following a meeting in Washington on 4 July 1999. Despite India's reluctance to cross the LoC, had its military operations in Kargil proven more difficult, there is a great probability that an additional front would have been opened to divert Pakistani resources. Also, during the Indian Air Force (IAF) air support operations, there were isolated incidences of IAF and PAF fighters locking their weapon systems on to one another. While no close air-to-air encounters took place, IAF Air Marshall Anil Tipnis confirmed that he had authorised his fighters to closely pursue PAF aircraft across the LoC if they were engaged by enemy aircraft in aerial combat.[36] While both sides may have sought to maintain a limited conflict, this outcome was far from certain. If operations had escalated horizontally beyond the Kargil region, a subsequent vertical escalation in intensity would have likely followed – thereby greatly increasing the potential for nuclear exchange. Playing out the dreadful possibilities led some scholars to conclude that the Kargil conflict revealed the limits of nuclear deterrence to demarcate, if not deter, a Pakistan–India conflict.[37]

Most of the media reports of missile mobilisation and mating of warheads emanated from Western sources. Bruce Riedel, who was present at the 4 July meeting between US President Clinton and Prime Minister Sharif at Blair House, wrote that Pakistan had readied its nuclear arsenal for a war.[38] Movement was also noticed by India. Although General V.P. Malik, chief of army staff during the conflict, said that India had no intelligence regarding the preparations of Pakistan's nuclear arsenal,[39] his successor reported in a 2001 interview that Pakistan had 'activated one of its nuclear missile bases and had threatened India with a nuclear attack'.[40]

An account of New Delhi's own nuclear preparations was detailed by a prominent Indian journalist, Raj Chengappa, who reported that during the conflict India had 'activated all its three types of nuclear delivery vehicles and kept them at ... Readiness 3 – meaning that some nuclear bombs were ready to be mated with the delivery vehicle on short notice; ... Mirage fighters were placed on standby; ... Prithvi missiles were deployed; [and] an Agni missile was moved ... and kept in a state of readiness.' Chengappa added that India had learnt that Pakistan had moved its nuclear weapons to an advanced state of readiness.[41]

All claims of nuclear preparations have been denied by Pakistani and Indian leadership. Musharraf called such specu-lations 'preposterous' and said that the notion that India and Pakistan were on the brink of nuclear war during the conflict was a 'myth'.[42] Feroz Khan has noted that during the last week of June – when US intelligence supposedly picked up Pakistani nuclear preparations – the director general of the Pakistani Strategic Plans Division was participating in arms-control negotiations in Geneva. Khan points to the unlikelihood that such preparations would have been made without the secretar-iat of the National Command Authority.[43] Some analysts have posited that the intelligence which confirmed such develop-ments possibly confused defensive relocation of nuclear assets for their operational deployment.[44]

2001–02 'Twin Peaks' crisis

With the restoration of the LoC and the military drawdown in the summer of 1999, the Kargil crisis came to an end. Despite the return to peacetime military deployments, however, tensions on the subcontinent remained high. Strained relations continued to be centred on Kashmir and the flow of militants across the LoC. In addition to sporadic attacks against civilians and security forces, militants hijacked an Indian airliner in December 1999 and carried out a suicide attack on the Jammu and Kashmir State Assembly building, killing 40 bystanders, in October 2001.

The increased violence in Kashmir was subsequently overshadowed by an assault on the Indian parliament in New Delhi on 13 December 2001. Fortunately, due to the unexpected adjournment of the parliamentary session earlier that day, the only casualties incurred were by the Indian security detail that confronted and killed the attackers.

Indian intelligence concluded that Pakistan-based terrorist groups Jaysh-e-Mohammad (JeM) and Lashkar-e-Taiba (LeT) were responsible for the attack and blamed Pakistan for complicity. In response, the Indian military initiated *Operation Parakram* – its largest mobilisation since the 1971 war – which included activating army strike formations with tanks and heavy artillery, deploying air-force squadrons to forward air bases near the border, and amassing naval assets in the Arabian Sea. Prime Minister Atal Bihari Vajpayee also recalled India's High Commissioner to Pakistan – the first time such a step had been taken by either country since the 1971 war. India demanded that Pakistan unequivocally renounce terrorism, extradite 20 suspected terrorists to India, shut down the militant training camps operating on Pakistani territory and stem the flow of militants across the LoC.

Fearing an Indian military strike, Pakistan responded with its own mobilisation, leading to roughly 1 million troops being deployed across the LoC and international border. While the Pakistani government publicly condemned the attack and offered a joint inquiry into the incident, it was unwilling to act on India's demands. By the new year, Indian forces had all appearances of being poised for attack; yet it remains unclear how close Indian leaders came to giving the green light for military action.

Tensions mounted as the stand-off continued. On 2 January 2002, at a meeting of the Joint Chiefs of Staff, Musharraf made a veiled nuclear threat, saying that contingency plans reflected a 'capacity of responding in a manner that would cause unacceptable damage to the enemy'.[45] That same day, speaking at an election rally, Vajpayee warned that 'no weapon would be spared in self-defence'.[46] Adding further risk of nuclear escalation, there were reports that both militaries had forward deployed short-range ballistic missiles that were nuclear capable.[47]

At the behest of US diplomats, Pakistan seemingly complied with India's demands. Musharraf banned five militant organisations, including LeT and JeM, placed their leaders under house arrest, froze some of the organisations' assets and arrested several hundred militants. In a public speech on 12 January, he promised that Pakistani territory would not be used to conduct terrorism in Kashmir. Musharraf also alluded to the possibility of extraditing 14 non-Pakistani suspects on India's terrorist list and said that the Pakistan military was ready to withdraw once India began moving its forces from the LoC/border.[48]

However, India remained unconvinced that these moves were anything more than political placation. Waiting for proof of a change in Pakistani policy, India retained its crisis-level deployment. Shortly after Musharraf's speech, the Defence Research and Development Organisation (DRDO) conducted a test of the new *Agni*-I ballistic missile. While this test may have been pre-scheduled and not meant as a show of force, the media coverage, which labelled the missile system as being Pakistan specific, was provocative. These likely unrelated events perpetuated an atmosphere of the subcontinent being on the edge of war.

On 14 May 2002, another terrorist attack (the second of the 'twin peaks') threatened to propel the situation over the edge. Three militants opened fire on a bus, then stormed the family quarters at an Indian Army camp in Kaluchak, located just outside Jammu City. The attack killed more than 30 people, including ten children. Blame was quickly laid on LeT. The general perception within India was that Pakistan had failed to live up to, or even ignored, the promises made by Musharraf. Many of the terrorists arrested after the 12 January speech had been released and training camps still operated openly.[49] The fact that Pakistan had just released the LeT leader from house arrest, promising to keep him under surveillance, further incited Indian anger. Three successive Pakistani ballistic-missile tests during the last week of May did little to reduce mounting tensions.

By the end of May, the two sides appeared to be on the brink of armed conflict. Several senior Pakistani officials reaffirmed earlier warnings by Musharraf that Pakistan might use nuclear weapons if it deemed its existence to be threatened. Indian Defence Minister George Fernandes famously responded that, 'we could take a strike, survive, and then hit back. Pakistan would be finished.'[50] Both Indian and Pakistani troops exchanged heavy artillery across the border and LoC, as well as conducting blackout drills in preparation for air-raid attacks. Preparing for the worst, Pakistan also held civil-defence and emergency-response drills in its eastern cities.

The seeming direness of the situation convinced the Pentagon to re-examine the effects of nuclear-weapons use in the subcontinent.[51] It also led US Ambassador to India Robert Blackwill to order the departure of all non-essential staff and dependents, exceeding the State Department's voluntary evacuation order. This move was followed by similar advisories from the British, Japanese, French, German, Israeli and other governments.

Despite heavy international pressure, Pakistan and India appeared unwilling or unable to defuse the crisis. However, following US Deputy Secretary of State Richard Armitage's visit to the region in early June, the situation finally began to de-escalate. On 6 June, Musharraf pledged to Armitage to 'visibly and permanently' end cross-border, cross-LoC militant infiltration.[52] Armitage then conveyed this pledge to Vajpayee along with US assurances that it would be honoured.[53]

According to Jaswant Singh's memoirs, there was never a nuclear dimension to the crisis in 2001–02.[54] Interviews with other senior political and military leaders from India suggest that the risk of nuclear escalation was perceived to be minimal. This position is seemingly supported by the absence of any reports claiming Pakistan had mated its warheads with their delivery systems during the crisis, despite the entire national-security apparatus being placed on high alert.[55]

However, several aspects of the stand-off support the notion that this crisis was the 'first real test of nuclear brinkmanship' between the two countries.[56] Unlike previous crises, nuclear sabre-rattling was overt and direct from the beginning and throughout the stand-off. Both countries had conducted ballistic-missile tests and deployed nuclear-capable missile systems. Furthermore, it is reported that the perceived threat of Indian attack led to Pakistan's testing of both dispersal and mating plans for its nuclear warheads.[57] That arsenal may have deterred India from responding forcefully to the attacks. But if India had gone forward with limited strikes, let alone the launching of a full-scale war as advocated by some in New Delhi, the crisis very possibly could have escalated to a nuclear exchange.

2008 Mumbai attack

On 26 November 2008, India again fell victim to a terrorist attack – this time in its largest city, Mumbai. Ten militants stole a small fishing vessel in southeast Pakistan and sailed to the city, where they broke into smaller groups to unleash almost 60 hours of terror. The attacks killed more than 170 people and injured more than 300. Intelligence quickly connected the assault to the LeT, identified the gunmen as Pakistani nationals and traced the launching of the operation back to Pakistani soil.

India demanded the extradition of 20 terrorist suspects, including several individuals Pakistan had failed to provide after India's similar request during the 2001–02 crisis. New Delhi also threatened air-strikes against LeT camps in Pakistan if Islamabad failed to take decisive action against the terrorist group. This prompted Islamabad to carry out a limited crackdown by arresting several LeT members – including two key associates involved in the planning of the Mumbai attack – and banning a LeT-affiliated charity, which quickly reopened under a new name.

International fears of an Indian reprisal and a subsequent escalation of the crisis mounted with growing evidence of Pakistan's Inter-Services Intelligence (ISI) involvement in the attack. Initial allegations were later reinforced by the US court testimony of Pakistani-American businessman-turned-militant David Headley. This fear was also evident in Pakistan, where the army and air force were placed on high alert, troops were redeployed from the eastern Pakistani border to the western one and military leave was cancelled.

However, New Delhi refrained from initiating any military action. Aside from some inflammatory rhetoric, the only incident of note concerned accusations of airspace violations by IAF fighter jets. Both militaries were able to conduct their annual military exercises that winter without the escalatory deployments prevalent in previous crises. The greatest impact of the crisis was its negative impact on diplomatic relations between the two countries. This was most visible in the suspension of the strategic 'Composite Dialogue', which was placed on hold until relations began to warm in 2011.

Assessment

The dominant Pakistani narrative regarding these five crises is that the nation was saved by its nuclear-weapons programme.[58] Indeed, strategic systems undoubtedly succeeded in signalling resolve. But they also contributed to misperceptions. In at least one of the cases (the 2001–02 crisis), South Asia arguably came close to a nuclear war. Riedel cautions that the next time may not turn out as lucky. At an April 2013 event in Washington, he said:

> We are heading towards the next crisis – it is only a matter of time. While people tend to minimise the potential for a new crisis or rationalise that a future crisis will not escalate into a nuclear exchange based on this history or previous crises, the best analogy is that of 'Russian roulette', and at some point there is going to be a bullet in the chamber.[59]

Underscoring such pessimism is the underdeveloped state of mechanisms for crisis resolution. Neither side appears to have learnt appropriate lessons of crisis management from the five crises described above. Communication channels are established then disused; as of 2014, the Composite Dialogue led by foreign ministers, and back-channel talks remain interrupted. When such talks have taken place, deterrence stability and the main factors that contribute to growing nuclear risks have not been on the agenda and military officers have played a limited role. Peripheral territorial disputes in the Siachen Glacier in the north and Sir Creek in the south that have long been ripe for resolution have been allowed to fester for decades. Track Two meetings between the two sides annually produce wise suggestions for confidence-building measures on which the governments cannot find common purpose. Washington's past role in mediating crises may no longer be as welcomed by a Pakistan that is so distrustful. A cabinet-level agreement in 2011 to extend mutual most-favoured nation (MFN) status remains unimplemented in Pakistan due to opposition by interest groups that fear losing out to Indian competition.

Leavening this pessimism are some positive trends in Indo-Pakistan relations. Notwithstanding several large-scale crises and many small-scale skirmishes, the ceasefire along the LoC has largely held since 2003. In 2012, agreements on pre-notification of flight testing of ballistic missiles and on reducing risks related to nuclear accidents were extended for another five years. The voluntary testing moratoria agreed in 1999 have been maintained. Unofficial discussions between retired senior officials have helped clear up misperceptions and misinterpretations.[60] Most importantly, India and Pakistan are increasing their economic ties, buoyed by an easing of visa restrictions. If MFN status is finally implemented, bilateral trade is expected to treble in three years.[61] Business communities on both sides have been vocal in insisting that prosperity requires peace. Regularising cross-border trade and investment is the most promising path for long-term peaceful relations.

Notes

[1] This conclusion is prevalent not just in Western circles but also in Russia. See Vladimir Radyuhin, 'Cold War Lessons for India and Pakistan', *The Hindu*, 19 November 2012.

[2] Mike Wooldridge, 'Analysis: Clinton's disappointments in South Asia', BBC News, 26 March 2000, http://news.bbc.co.uk/1/hi/world/south_asia/691339.stm.

3 George Perkovich, comments at meeting on 'Challenges to Strategic Stability in Southern Asia', Carnegie Endowment for International Peace, 1 October 2012.

4 Kenneth Waltz, 'The Spread of Nuclear Weapons: More May Be Better', Adelphi Paper 171 (London: International Institute for Strategic Studies, 1981).

5 S. Paul Kapur, 'India and Pakistan's Unstable Peace: Why Nuclear South Asia Is Not Like Cold War Europe', *International Security*, vol. 30, no. 2, Fall 2005, pp. 127–52.

6 Michael Krepon, 'The Stability-Instability Paradox, Misperception and Escalation Control in South Asia', in Michael Krepon, Rodney W. Jones and Ziad Haider (eds), *Escalation Control and the Nuclear Option in South Asia* (Washington DC: Stimson Center, 2004), http://www.stimson.org/books-reports/escalation-control-and-the-nuclear-option-in-south-asia-/. See also Iskander Rehman, 'Drowning Stability: The Perils of Naval Nuclearization and Brinkmanship in the Indian Ocean', *Naval War College Review*, vol. 65, no. 4, Autumn 2012, pp. 64–88, http://www.usnwc.edu/getattachment/187a93e1-db4c-474e-9be8-038bb7a64edb/Drowning-Stability--The-Perils-of-Naval-Nucleariza.aspx.

7 Scott D. Sagan, *The Limits of Safety* (Princeton, NJ: Princeton University Press, 1995).

8 Michael J. Boyle, 'The costs and consequences of drone warfare', *International Affairs*, vol. 89, no. 1, January 2013, pp. 19–20.

9 The South Asia Terrorism Portal website lists 44 terrorist and extremist groups in Pakistan. http://www.satp.org/satporgtp/countries/Pakistan/terroristoutfits/group_list.htm. David Smith estimates that 50–60 active or partially active terrorist groups operate in Pakistan. David O. Smith, 'The US Experience with Tactical Nuclear Weapons: Lessons for South Asia', Stimson Center, 4 March 2013, http://www.stimson.org/images/uploads/research-pdfs/David_Smith_Tactical_Nuclear_Weapons.pdf.

10 George Perkovich, 'The Non-Unitary Model And Deterrence Stability In South Asia', Stimson Center, 13 November 2012, http://www.stimson.org/images/uploads/research-pdfs/George_Perkovich_-_The_Non_Unitary_Model_and_Deterrence_Stability_in_South_Asia.pdf.

11 Pakistani attitudes were inflamed by: a 27 January 2011 incident in which CIA contractor Raymond Davis killed two civilians and a third died during a US attempt to aid Davis; the 2 May 2011 US Navy SEALs raid on Osama bin Laden's compound in Abbottabad; and the 26 November 2011 misbegotten NATO attack on a Pakistani border checkpoint at Salala that resulted in 24 Pakistani military deaths.

12 The author is indebted to Daniel Painter for drafting the following histories.

13 The LoC was established by the Simla Agreement that ended the 1971 war.

14 Michael Krepon and Nate Cohn (eds), 'Crises in South Asia: Trends and Potential Consequences', Stimson Center, September 2011, pp. 30–31, http://www.stimson.

org/images/uploads/research-pdfs/
Crises_Complete.pdf.

15 *Ibid.* For a detailed background, see
Kanti Bajpai et al., *Brasstacks and
Beyond: Perception and Management
of Crisis in South Asia* (New Delhi:
Manohar, 1995); and P.R. Chari,
Pervaiz Iqbal Cheema and Steven
Cohen, *Four Crises and a Peace
Process: American Engagement
in South Asia* (Washington DC:
Brookings Institution Press, 2007).

16 See Scott D. Sagan, 'More Will
Be Worse', in Scott D. Sagan and
Kenneth N. Waltz, *The Spread of
Nuclear Weapons: A Debate Renewed*
(New York: W.W. Norton & Co.,
2003) and Feroz H. Khan, *Eating
Grass: The Making of the Pakistani
Bomb* (Stanford, CA: Stanford
University Press, 2012), p. 222.

17 S. Paul Kapur, *Dangerous Deterrent:
Nuclear Weapons Proliferation and
Conflict in South Asia* (Stanford, CA:
Stanford University Press, 2007),
pp. 86–87.

18 Kuldip Nayar, 'Has Pakistan really
joined the nuclear bomb club?',
Globe and Mail, 2 March 1987.

19 Khan, *Eating Grass*, p. 225.

20 Kargil Review Committee Report,
23 February 2000, p. 191.

21 Sumit Ganguly and S. Paul Kapur,
*India, Pakistan, and the Bomb: Debating
Nuclear Stability in South Asia* (New
York: Columbia University Press,
2007), p. 40.

22 George Perkovich, *India's Nuclear
Bomb: The Impact on Global
Proliferation* (Berkeley, CA:
University of California Press,
1999), p. 13.

23 US Deputy Secretary of Defense
Paul Wolfowitz stated that the
US knew Pakistan had assembled

a nuclear weapon following an
intercepted PAEC message – cited
by George Perkovich, *India's
Nuclear Bomb: The Impact on Global
Proliferation* (New Delhi: Oxford
University Press, 2000), pp. 308–9.
General Naseerullah also claimed
weapon assembly in an interview
reported in Mary Ann Weaver,
*Pakistan: In the Shadow of Jihad and
Afghanistan* (New York: Farrar,
Straus & Giroux, 2003), p. 206.

24 Seymour Hersh said the convoys left
the storage facility in Baluchistan.
Seymour M. Hersh, 'On the Nuclear
Edge', *New Yorker*, 29 March 1993,
pp. 64–65; whereas John Adams
claimed they left Khan Research
Laboratories (KRL). John Adams,
'Pakistan Nuclear War Threat',
Sunday Times, 27 May 1990.

25 Khan, *Eating Grass*, pp. 230–31.

26 Vipin Narang, 'Posturing for Peace?
Pakistan's Nuclear Postures and
South Asian Stability', *International
Security*, vol. 34, no. 3, p. 52.

27 Hersh, 'On the Nuclear Edge', pp.
64–65.

28 Feroz Kahn, 'Prospects for Indian
and Pakistani Arms Control', in
Henry Sokolski (ed.), *The Next Arms
Race* (Carlisle, PA: Strategic Studies
Institute, U.S. Army War College,
2012), p. 368.

29 Kapur, *Dangerous Deterrent*, pp.
110–13.

30 See, for example, Narang, 'Posturing
for Peace?', p. 52; Gen. Beg told
Feroz Khan that the nuclear devices
were assembled and placed on
aircraft to trigger US intervention
to prevent an Indo-Israeli assault
against KRL.

31 Kapur, *Dangerous Deterrent*, pp.
112–23.

32 Pervez Hoodbhoy, 'Pakistan: Understanding the "World's Fastest Growing Arsenal"', in Pervez Hoodbhoy (ed.), *Confronting the Bomb: Pakistani and Indian Scientists Speak Out* (Karachi: Oxford University Press, 2013), p. 107.

33 Pervez Musharraf, *In the Line of Fire: A Memoir* (New York: Free Press, 2008), p. 97.

34 Throughout the conflict, Pakistan maintained the operation was undertaken by mujahideen, not the Pakistani military. However, phone calls intercepted by Indian intelligence implicated the Pakistan military. Pakistani Lt.-Gen. (Retd) Shahid Aziz, who headed the ISI's analysis wing during the conflict, recently stated that the forces were entirely comprised of Pakistani regulars. Shahid Aziz, 'Putting our children in line of fire', *Nation*, 6 January 2013.

35 Usman Ghani, 'Nuclear Weapons in India–Pakistan Crisis', IPRI Journal XII, no. 2, Summer 2012, pp. 141–42.

36 Air Commodore Kaiser Tufail (Retd), 'Kargil 1999: The PAF's Story', *Vayu Aerospace and Defense Review*, no. 3, 2009.

37 Chari, Cheema and Cohen, *Four Crises and a Peace Process*, p. 140.

38 Bruce Riedel, 'American Diplomacy and the 1999 Kargil Summit at Blair House', Center for the Advanced Study of India, Policy Paper Series, 2002.

39 V.P. Malik, *Kargil: From Surprise to Victory* (New Delhi: Harper Collins, 2006), pp. 259–60.

40 Raj Chengappa interview with General Sundararajan Padmanabhan, 'Pakistan Threatened India with Nuclear Attack during Kargil War: Army Chief', *News Today*, 12 January 2001, cited in John H. Gill, 'Military operations in the Kargil conflict', in Peter R. Lavoy (ed.), *Asymmetrical Warfare in South Asia: The Causes and Consequences of the Kargil Conflict* (Cambridge: Cambridge University Press, 2009), p. 112.

41 Raj Chengappa, *Weapons of Peace* (New Delhi: HarperCollins India, 2000), pp. 436–38.

42 Musharraf, *In the Line of Fire*, p. 98.

43 Khan, *Eating Grass*, p. 315.

44 Timothy D. Hoyt, 'Kargil: the nuclear dimension', in Lavoy (ed.), *Asymmetrical Warfare in South Asia*, p. 159.

45 'JCSC reviews counter-strategy', *Dawn*, 2 January 2002.

46 J.P. Shukla, 'No weapon will be spared for self-defence: PM', *The Hindu*, 3 January 2002.

47 Chari, Cheema and Cohen, *Four Crises and a Peace Process*, p. 173; and 'India's missile system in position: Fernandes', *The Hindu*, 27 December 2001.

48 Alan Sipress and Rajiv Chandrasekran, 'Powell "Encouraged" by India Visit; New Delhi Officials Signal Approval of Pakistani Crackdown on Islamic Militants', *Washington Post*, 19 January 2002.

49 Krepon and Cohn (eds), 'Crises in South Asia', p. 48.

50 Pervez Hoodbhoy, 'India–Pakistan: What, Us Worry?', *Los Angeles Times*, 9 June 2002.

51 Polly Nayak and Michael Krepon, *US Crisis Management in South Asia's Twin Peaks Crisis* (Washington DC: Stimson Center, 2006), p. 33.

52 *Ibid.*, pp. 35–36; Chari, Cheema and Cohen, *Four Crises and a Peace Process*, p. 163.

53 Kapur, *Dangerous Deterrent*, p. 135.

54 Jaswant Singh, *A Call to Honour: In Service of Emergent India* (New Delhi: Rupa and Co., 2006), p. 341.

55 Peter Lavoy, 'Pakistan's Nuclear Posture: Security and Survivability', paper presented to the Conference on Pakistan's Nuclear Future, Non-proliferation Education Center, Washington DC, 28 April 2006, p. 11, http://www.npolicy.org/files/20070121-Lavoy-PakistanNuclearPosture.pdf.

56 Adil Sultan, 'Pakistan's emerging nuclear posture: impact of drivers and technology on nuclear doctrine', Institute of Strategic Studies Islamabad, 17 April 2012, p. 157.

57 Naveeda Kahn, *Beyond Crisis: Re-evaluating Pakistan* (New Delhi: Routledge India, 2010), p. 280.

58 Agha Shahi, Zulfiqar Ali Khan and Abdul Sattar, 'Securing nuclear peace', *News International*, 5 October 1999; Musharraf, *In the Line of Fire*, p. 286; and Shamshad Ahmad, 'A South Asian Reality', *News International*, 28 May 2012.

59 Bruce Riedel, Hudson Institute event, 'Avoiding Armageddon: America, India, Pakistan, to the Brink and Back', 17 April 2013.

60 V.R. Raghavan, 'Views on Nuclear Risks in South Asia', presentation at the American Association for the Advancement of Science, 18 October 2012, http://www.stimson.org/images/uploads/research-pdfs/Reducing_Nuclear_Risks_in_South_Asia_-_Raghavan.pdf.

61 'MFN status can boost Indo-Pak trade to $6b', *Express Tribune*, 12 December 2012.

CHAPTER THREE

The potential for a nuclear arms race

Although the potential for nuclear terrorism garners more media attention, the nuclear-arms competition in South Asia is of greater concern. As discussed in Chapter Four, Pakistan understands the terrorism problem and has taken steps to address nuclear-security vulnerabilities. As discussed in this chapter, equivalent steps have not been taken to stop a budding nuclear and missile arms race. Officials in India and Pakistan rarely even admit to the problem. However, the facts plainly indicate that nuclear competition is intensifying.

The South Asian arms race has a complexion of its own, different in many respects from the US–USSR Cold War competition – which at its peak in 1985 reached over 62,000 bombs in total. Together, the India and Pakistan arsenals comprise less than a third of 1% of that number. Their competition is less about numbers than about competing capabilities, both conventional and nuclear, although asymmetries in certain capabilities can produce a numerical race too, as a means of compensation. Unlike the Cold War, the South Asian arms race is three-dimensional, with China's nuclear arsenal a key factor. The China factor also amplifies a unidirectional aspect of the race, with India seeking to catch up with China, and Pakistan in turn aiming to catch up with India – although Pakistani decisions can also affect Indian plans.

Whereas the United States and Russia continue to reduce their arsenals, India and Pakistan are moving in the opposite direction. They are not trying to match numbers of weapons, nor even trying to match every system introduced by the other. However, both nations are expanding their fissile-material production capabilities and the variety and sophistication of their delivery platforms. American academic Paul Bracken notes that this competition in sub-systems presents more danger than a competition in numbers because it lends itself less easily to arms-control agreements.[1] In Western capitals there is particular concern that the introduction of tactical nuclear weapons (TNW) lowers the nuclear-use threshold, making nuclear war more likely. According to one recent study, such a war in South Asia could kill 20 million people in the first week and put up to 2 billion people at risk of famine globally.[2]

The strategic communities in South Asia, both in and outside government, adopt a less worried air and insist that they have no intention of engaging in an arms race. Being at a growing financial disadvantage, Pakistan has more reason to disavow a costly arms competition. India, seeing itself as an extra-regional power with more pressing concerns vis-à-vis China, rejects all notions of bilateral competition with Pakistan. In both countries, there is a sense of nonchalance about the dangers of nuclear war.

To the extent that they recognise an arms competition, Pakistan and India place the blame entirely on each other. Pakistani officials insist that India's 'Cold Start' doctrine sparked their own battlefield-use nuclear posture and 'modest' upgrades in deterrence. They also complain that India has spurned all of Pakistan's efforts since 1998 to establish a strategic restraint regime and various confidence-building measures that Pakistan has proposed. Indian officials blame Pakistan for repeated terrorist attacks that sparked Indian moves to restore conventional deterrence. They complain that Pakistan's introduction of TNWs has upset the deterrence equation.[3]

Based on estimated weapons numbers, Pakistan is currently winning the race. It is estimated to have at least ten more bombs than India (as of January 2013, 100–120 vs 90–110, according to the Stockholm International Peace Research Institute)[4] and, as noted in Chapter One, to be producing enough enriched uranium and plutonium every year for about 10 bombs, compared to about half that for India at present.[5] Pakistan's annual production will soon rise to about 16. The effort is more than a sprint; the expansion in fissile-material production capabilities will enable weapons growth for many years.

While Pakistan is increasing its nuclear-weapons arsenal at a faster pace, India has a much greater inherent advantage in terms of dual-use facilities that could be put to military purpose. As of 2013, India's weapons programme mainly relied on the 100MWt Dhruva reactor, which can produce 11–18kg of plutonium a year or 2–3 weapons' worth. The 40MWt CIRUS (Canadian–Indian, US) reactor, which had also been used for producing weapons-grade plutonium, was shut down at the end of 2010 in accordance with the US–India nuclear-cooperation agreement. India can also produce about 3–4 weapons' worth of highly enriched uranium (HEU) every year from its enrichment facility at the Rare Materials Plant near Mysore,[6] but most of its present enrichment output is believed to be for fuel for naval and research reactors.[7]

Plutonium for weapons purposes can be produced by any reactor, including the fast-breeder reactors (FBR) that remain outside safeguards under the terms of the US–India nuclear-cooperation deal. The first prototype 500MWe FBR at

Kalpakkam, which is scheduled to come online in September 2014, could produce up to 140kg of weapons-grade pluto-nium a year.[8] India insists that its FBR will be used for power generation, but it has acknowledged that keeping them outside safeguards was 'for maintaining the minimum credible deter-rent',[9] meaning they might also need to be used for weapons. Five other FBRs are under construction.[10] Pakistan has no FBRs and no unsafeguarded power reactors.

India is also expanding its reprocessing capabilities, which are unsafeguarded even though most of them are used for civilian purposes. As of 2013, India had four reprocessing plants, with a combined capacity to reprocess 350 tonnes of spent fuel a year. Another 100-tonne capacity will be added with the completion of a second plant at Kalpakkam in 2014, and there are plans for additional plants to add close to 500 tonnes per year.[11] India is also expanding its uranium-enrichment programme by adding a second gas centrifuge facility at the Rare Materials Plant. Another Special Material Enrichment Facility is also planned for the Chitradurga district in Karnataka, although construction was temporarily halted in summer 2013.[12] These new capabilities could double India's current 15,000–30,000 SWU enrichment capacity, allowing it to produce 7–15 HEU weapons a year.

In addition to expanding its fissile-material production capacities, India is also developing a more diversified and robust triad of land-, air- and sea-based delivery platforms. A June 2012 meeting of India's Nuclear Command Authority reportedly urged a 'faster consolidation' of India's nuclear-deterrence posture.[13] Already, in July 2011 India had newly tested a 150km-range *Prahaar* short-range ballistic missile (SRBM). The 350km *Prithvi*-II SRBM has been tested eight times since 2011 and its *Dhanush* naval variant twice. The submarine-launched 700km *Sangarika* (also known as K-15 or B-05) was tested for the twelfth time in December 2012 then declared to be operational and ready to be integrated with the nuclear-powered *Arihant* submarine. In August 2013, the submarine was pronounced ready for sea trials, with its reactor having gone critical. In March 2013, India tested a submarine variant of the 290km *BrahMos* supersonic cruise missile from an underwater pontoon. In March 2013, the *Nirbhay* 1,000km subsonic cruise missile was tested from a surface platform and is to be inducted into the Indian Army, Navy and Air Force. In the past two years, additional test launches have been conducted of the 700km *Agni*-I SRBM, the 2,000km *Agni*-II medium-range ballistic missile (MRBM) and the 3,000km *Agni*-III MRBM. Avinash Chander, the new head of India's Defence Research and Development Organisation (DRDO), revealed in a July 2013 interview that he had a mandate to drastically reduce the time it would take India to deliver a nuclear counter-strike.[14]

In November 2011, India successfully tested a solid-fuelled 4,000km-range *Agni*-IV ballistic missile. In April 2012 and September 2013, an *Agni*-V intercontinental ballistic missile with an estimated range of 5,500–5,800km was tested. The latter two long-range missiles are more relevant strategically to China than to Pakistan, which is more concerned about accuracy and payload than the range of India's missiles. India has three types of nuclear-capable aircraft and has announced an intention to purchase 126 new fighter-bombers from France. The DRDO also claims to be developing multiple independently targetable re-entry vehicle (MIRV) technology.[15] To do so, however, India would also need to develop smaller weapons that would enable multiple warheads to fit into a single missile nose cone.

Another Indian priority is the development of ballistic-missile defences (BMD), which could further shift the strategic balance in India's favour. In June 2013, the DRDO announced completion of the first phase of a BMD system that can target missiles at a range of up to 2,000km. A second phase, claimed to be in advanced stages of development, aims to extend that range to 5,000km.[16] Taking all these developments into account, American political scientist Vipin Narang concludes that 'India is developing a range of potential capabilities that could allow it to one day adopt a counterforce or escalation dominance strategy over Pakistan.'[17]

India's defence capabilities are designed with two adversaries in mind, with China being given more attention than Pakistan. It was China's aggression and defeat of Indian forces in the 1962 border war and China's nuclear test two years later that sparked India's own nuclear-weapons programme. China's nuclear forces and expanding naval reach are driving the advances in India's strategic technologies. In recent years, India has also claimed increased incursions by China across the disputed border.[18] From an outside perspective, India's concerns about China seem overstated. Although China officially claims the entire state of Arunachal Pradesh and large areas of Aksai Chin in the west, its actual objectives in the scarcely populated mountain areas are limited. Nuclear weapons have little role in such low-intensity skirmishes. And India appears to play a marginal role in China's nuclear posture and military modernisation, which are directed mainly with the US and its allies in mind. Nevertheless, India fears that, without a nuclear deterrent, it would be unable to respond if China became more aggressive, and it sees Chinese missile build-ups in Tibet as especially threatening. The China factor thus complicates any efforts to stem the arms competition between India and Pakistan.

As with the DRDO's MIRV aspiration, smaller warheads would also be needed were India to use the 420mm-diameter *Prahaar* SRBM for nuclear weapons. Indian officials have not claimed that the *Prahaar* is nuclear capable, only that it can carry 'different types of warheads'.[20] When the DRDO called the export version a 'counter-force' weapon at an arms fair in Seoul in October 2013,[21] it may not have intended the nuclear-deterrent meaning of counterforce.

In fact, India denies any intention to introduce TNWs at all, since they are incompatible with its policies of no first use and massive retaliation in response to any nuclear attack. Not persuaded and looking at the worst-case scenario, Pakistan assumes that India has already developed a TNW strategy of its own, in order to have a more flexible response to Pakistan's battlefield nuclear strategy. The *Prahaar* is seen in this light.[22] At present, this assessment is exaggerated, given that India's smallest nuclear weapon is over twice the weight of the 200kg warhead capacity of the *Prahaar*. There are suspicions that India's DRDO is interested in TNWs, however, and is report-edly already seeking to miniaturise warheads for MIRV ballistic missiles.[23]

Small nuclear warheads may also be under development for the *Nirbhay* and *BrahMos* cruise missiles. Russia, with whom India has been jointly developing the *BrahMos*, has called the system nuclear capable, although India itself has not labelled it dual use.[24] Former US defence attaché David Smith counts 11 short-range systems under development by India that 'could easily be modified to carry nuclear warheads'.[25]

Most Indian strategists support the Indian government's position on rejecting TNWs. Observing the lessons of TNWs in the Cold War, retired Indian Lt.-Gen. V.R. Raghavan opines that these weapons were proven to be 'burdensome, to compli-cate planning, and to be useless'.[26] Retired Brig. Gurmeet Kanwal concludes: 'Since no major advantages seem to accrue from tactical nuclear weapons in future conflicts on the Indian Subcontinent, their development and introduction into service are best avoided. The Indian nuclear arsenal does not need tactical nuclear weapons – and never will.'[27] A minority of Indian analysts argue, to the contrary, that a range of nuclear options along the ladder of escalation would enhance the credibility of India's nuclear deterrent.[28]

In addition to these strategic systems, India has superior conventional forces, with more than a 2–1 advantage in numbers and a growing edge in technology. India's quantitative advantage is offset by its need also to deploy forces in its northeast against China. Given mobilisation times, Indian superiority would take weeks to make itself felt.[19] Pakistan assumes the worst case, however, and contrasts total numbers. By every comparison, therefore, Pakistan sees itself at a growing disadvantage.

Pakistan's motivations for TNWs

In the early years of the twenty-first century, Pakistan suddenly saw the strategic equilibrium that had prevailed in the first decade of the South Asia nuclear age shifting dramatically in India's favour. A variety of developments contributed to this perception, including India's faster economic growth and conventional military build-up, both of which had been in play for some years. In the new century, however, two new factors suddenly emerged. The first was the Cold Start terrorism-response plan, developed by the Indian Army as a means for a quick and limited conventional attack that would not cross Pakistan's ambiguous nuclear red lines. The second was the US–India nuclear-cooperation deal, which would give India an edge in nuclear technology and, as a by-product, make nuclear materials available for weapons use. India's quest for missile defence and other advanced capabilities were additional reasons for concern. Pakistan perceived the prospect of growing asymmetry in both the conventional and strategic spheres. Its attempt to re-level the playing field was

Source: Masood Ur Rehman Khattak, 'Indian Military's Cold Start Doctrine: Capabilities, Limitations and Possible Response from Pakistan', SASSI Research Paper 32, March 2011, p. 10, http://www.sassi.org/wp-content/uploads/2012/05/RP-32-Masood-Indian-Militarys-Cold-Start-Doctrine-Mar-2011.pdf. Used with permission of South Asian Strategic Stability Institute.   © IISS

Map 2. **Possible thrusts of Indian integrated battle groups (IBG) under 'Cold Start' doctrine**

to lower the nuclear threshold through the introduction of TNWs.

Frustrated by the military stand-off that prevented *Operation Parakram* from succeeding in 'punishing' Pakistan for the December 2001 terrorist attack on the Indian parliament and worried about the impact on their ability to deter such attacks in the future, the Indian Army developed a plan for rapid mobilisation of forces that could make limited incursions across the border. Calibrating the retaliation was key; it would need to be large enough to deter future acts of terrorism but not so large as to provoke a nuclear response. Announced in April 2004, the plan, one element of which was labelled Cold Start, called for the formation of 8–10 integrated battle groups able to cross the border within 72–96 hours, then to penetrate 30–40 miles into Pakistani territory. British political scientist Shashank Joshi notes that this distance is 'almost certainly exaggerated and/or speculative', as well as being problematic because key population centres and communication lines lie within that distance of the border.[29] Yet the threat of a 30–40 mile (48–64km) incursion has taken root in the Pakistani psyche and is emphasised in threat briefings, often rounded up to 50–70km[30] and even to 90km, depending on the sub-theatre.[31]

Despite the widespread attention it has attracted, Cold Start has never been adopted by the Indian military as a whole nor endorsed by India's civilian leadership. In fact, it has been disavowed.[32] Western scholars who have assessed India's supposed doctrinal change have called Cold Start 'more of a concept than a reality'[33] and 'a non-starter for a number of political, diplomatic, logistical and tactical reasons'.[34] Calling it a 'doctrine stillborn', Joshi in 2013 outlined five sets of structural obstacles to India's ability to put Cold Start in place. The obstacles include the persistence of nuclear constraints, civilian resistance, inter-service rivalry, general unreadiness and the burden of new military tasks.[35] Even if India's political leadership were to agree to the doctrine, it would take 20 years to be effectively implemented, one respected Indian analyst has written.[36]

The persistent nuclear shadow now associated with Cold Start may be the most compelling reason why Indian leaders are unlikely to give the green light for such a cross-border attack. One might say that Pakistan's battlefield nuclear posture has already served its deterrent purpose by discouraging India from following through with the army's grand plan. But there was never much political support for it anyway.

Speaking at a seminar in December 2013, a senior Pakistani official insisted that 'as of today, Cold Start is an active operational doctrine.' As evidence, he pointed to railway and road networks and munitions stockpiles in place, as well as training and Indian Army–Air Force coordination.[37] Large-scale manoeuvres by the Indian armed forces in 2006 were described by Indian Army officers themselves in reference to the 2004 doctrine.[38] When the Indian Army in 2012 began using the term 'proactive defence',[39] it was seen in Pakistan as an ill-disguised euphemism for the same plan for integrated battle-group attacks across the border. Yet proactive defence encompasses more than this.

India has more than one way of responding forcefully to another terrorist attack emanating from Pakistan. India is shifting its focus to stand-off capabilities that do not require personnel to cross the border, including via cruise missiles or the cheaper Joint Direct Attack Munitions (bomb guidance kits). Targeted missile strikes against jihadist headquarters or training camps held responsible for terrorist attacks should not trigger a Pakistani nuclear response. However small-scale the nuclear weapon used, it would be a hugely disproportionate response to a limited conventional strike, especially one that was against non-governmental targets.

Pakistani strategists cite Cold Start as the primary reason that their nation developed TNWs. Introducing the short-range missile is seen as the way to restore nuclear deterrence. In Lt.-Gen. (Retd) Khalid Kidwai's words, the intent of the short-range systems is to 'pour cold water on Cold Start'.[40] There is no reason to doubt that this is the case with the *Nasr*, given its recent vintage. However, Cold Start cannot have been the trigger for the development of Pakistan's first short-range nuclear-armed missile, the *Abdali*. As noted in Chapter One, the *Abdali* was first flight tested in 2002 and its dual-use purpose was announced a year later, before Cold Start itself was announced.

The second major stimulus to Pakistan's new nuclear doctrine was the US decision in 2005 to lift a long-standing prohibition on nuclear cooperation with India. The US–India nuclear deal, announced by President George W. Bush and Prime Minister Manmohan Singh during a July 2005 summit in Washington, overturned decades of a US non-proliferation policy that required adherence to the Nuclear Non-Proliferation Treaty (NPT) as a condition for nuclear export. The condition was also enshrined in the guidelines of the Nuclear Suppliers Group (NSG), which was formed in response to India's 1974 nuclear test. To consummate the deal, the US Congress had to revise domestic US law and the NSG had to agree to an exemption – steps that were not completed until October 2008. India agreed to distinguish between its civil and military nuclear facilities and to place all of the former facilities under International Atomic Energy Agency (IAEA) safeguards. Fourteen nuclear power plants were designated as civilian, leaving eight others, including five still under construction, outside safeguards and thus potentially available for military use. If dedicated to weapons-grade plutonium production, they could produce up to 400 weapons' worth a year.[41]

The deal stoked Pakistani concerns on two levels. Firstly, it was seen to threaten national security. The number of nuclear facilities left unsafeguarded was staggering; even if not used for weapons purposes, leaving them outside the purely civilian designation signalled India's potential for a rapid increase in plutonium production. In addition, Pakistan judged that allowing India to import uranium ore would free up its limited domestic uranium resources for military use. The benefit gained by India in this respect is minor, given the small amount of uranium needed for weapons in comparison to the amount needed to fuel nuclear power plants, but the perception of unfair advantage cannot be shaken. The deal also threatened national pride. Pakistan fumed at the unfairness of its rival uniquely receiving the exemption, which could not be offered to Pakistan due to its poor record of nuclear stewardship, as explained in Chapter Five. The deal was seen as a US tilt toward India and a further abandonment of a long-suffering ally. More recent talk about possible US–India cooperation in BMD[42] exacerbates Pakistan's insecurities.

International cooperation with India's civil nuclear programme will not directly assist its military programme, as long as IAEA safeguards are in place. In the short term, importing uranium could allow India to reallocate fuel to reactors used for military purposes, although there is no indication that India has any intention of doing this. New discoveries of uranium deposits in India will further reduce any indirect military advantage that India might gain from the NSG waiver. The perceptions unleashed by the exemption, however, have already created their own negative momentum in Pakistan.

Both Khushab-3 and -4 were started after the US–India nuclear deal. Although plans for Khushab-3 probably predated 2005, there is clear evidence that Khushab-4 was decided upon in 2006 in reaction to the agreement.[43] The deal may also have triggered a decision to veto multilateral negotiation of a Fissile Material Cut-off Treaty (FMCT).

Pakistani strategists cite India's conventional-force build-up as a third motivation for expanding Pakistan's nuclear arsenal.[44] The growing asymmetry in conventional-weapons technology and military spending between the two countries weighs heavily on Pakistani minds. David Smith notes that, 'India's massive military modernization program is eroding the reasonable conventional military balance that Pakistan has traditionally relied on to deter war.'[45] TNWs are the new equaliser.

India's trumpeted advances in strategic systems and announcements about BMD demonstrations and emerging

MIRV capabilities further stimulate the arms-race dynamic. In May 2013, a Pakistan Foreign Office spokesman said the nation's short-range missiles were meant to address India's increasing conventional-weapons asymmetry, its offensive doctrine and its development of a BMD system.[46] One possible response to India's BMD programme is for Pakistan to consider MIRV capabilities of its own, as well as missile-defence countermeasures.[47] But this is a competition Pakistan cannot win, given India's much larger defence R&D budget.

Destabilising impact of TNWs

Concerns about the potentially destabilising impact of a nuclear arms race in South Asia have been heightened by Pakistan's introduction of battlefield nuclear weapons. Pakistan does not itself call the *Nasr* and *Abdali* systems TNWs. It recognises that the use of any nuclear weapon in South Asia would have a strategic effect.[48] The Strategic Plans Division (SPD) describes the systems as 'short-range, low-yield weapons'. In effect, however, they have the main characteristics associated with TNWs: their range, size and doctrine make them most suitable for use on the battlefield involving conventional military forces. For convenience's sake, let us continue to call them tactical or battlefield-use weapons.

Deployment of TNWs can lead to rapid escalation if deterrence fails. American nuclear-strategy scholar Robert Jervis in 1984 described the ever-present dangers of undesired escalation in nuclear crisis:

> The room for misunderstanding, the pressure to act before the other side has seized the initiative, the role of unexpected defeats or unanticipated opportunities, all are sufficiently great – and interacting – so that it is rare that decision-makers can confidently predict the

end point of the trajectory which an initial resort to violence starts.[49]

Battlefield TNWs compound the dangers of escalation because the shorter distances involved can easily make for a fateful 'use them or lose them' choice for the local commander. In enumerating the risks, US security scholar Rodney Jones argues that despite camouflage, the *Nasr* system will be easily identifiable to attacking forces because of its distinct signature of each transporter-erector launcher (TEL) and accompanying systems and thus would be a high-priority target for detection and pre-emptive air attack.[50] It is not hard to anticipate scenarios where a nuclear escalation is prompted by an effort to avoid loss of the weapons, particularly given India's seemingly relaxed attitude to targeting delivery systems with conventional means.

Indeed, in another manifestation of the stability/instability paradox, Pakistan wants to foster an environment where there is fear of rapid escalation.[51] Pakistani strategists depend exclusively on deterrence. If the *Nasr* restores the credibility of the nation's deterrence and strategic equilibrium, then concerns about command and control and strategic stability are less relevant, they argue.[52] From their perspective, the *Nasr* is a 'weapon of peace' because it adds to deterrence stability by deterring limited war.[53] Taking a page from NATO deterrence theorists such as Michael Quinlan,[54] SPD Arms Control and Disarmament Director Adil Sultan argues that 'war prevention needs to operate at all levels of military conflict between nuclear-capable states and not only at the strategic level.'[55] 'Full spectrum deterrence' is a qualitative rather than quantitative shift. Zahir Kazmi, also of the SPD Arms Control and Disarmament Directorate, writes that 'if Nasr forecloses India's dangerous option to fight a limited war under nuclear overhang, it contributes to the regional stability and makes Pakistan's deterrence more credible.' He acknowledges that deterrence will be problematic if India disbelieves Pakistan's will to use short-range nuclear weapons, but he implies that India's move away from Cold Start indicates that India takes Pakistan's nuclear resolve seriously.[56] Like most other Pakistani analysts, he does not acknowledge the circumstances that might trigger India's resort to an attack on Pakistani territory.

Pakistani officials argue that nuclear escalation could be controlled and that the use of one or two small battlefield-use nuclear weapons would compel Indian attackers to retreat.[57] It seems just as likely, however, that escalation rather than de-escalation would ensue. India has underscored its policy that it would respond with 'massive punitive retaliation', which is to say nuclear force, to any nuclear attack on its personnel, whether they are in or outside Indian territory.[58] Former foreign secretary Shyam Saran, convener of the National Security Advisory Board, an official consultative body of non-governmental experts, spelt it out clearly in a forceful speech in April 2013:[59]

> India will not be the first to use nuclear weapons, but if it is attacked with such weapons, it would engage in nuclear retaliation which will be massive and designed to inflict unacceptable damage on its adversary. The label on a nuclear weapon used for attacking India, strategic or tactical, is irrelevant from the Indian perspective.[60]

Pakistani officials and many outside observers consider claims that India would resort to such nuclear escalation strikes as not credible,[61] but there is no saying for sure. Having insisted that massive retaliation would be its response to low-yield nuclear use by an adversary, India conceivably could fall prey to a commitment trap whereby it feels forced to follow through in order to maintain deterrence because of past assertions. Pakistan is susceptible to the same dangerous dynamic. To maintain the credibility of its claims, it may feel bound to use low-yield nuclear weapons against an Indian cross-border incursion that falls well short of threatening Pakistan's vital interests.[62]

Strain on command and control

New capabilities are also driving changes in Pakistan's nuclear posture with regard to alert status. Unlike the nuclear stand-off between the superpowers, neither India nor Pakistan has had nuclear weapons on hair-trigger alert. Their weapons are understood not to be mated with delivery systems and not operationally deployed.[63] This 'recessed deployment' may be reinforced in Pakistan's case, and perhaps India's as well,[64] by the fissile core being stored separately from the rest of the weapon device, although the evidence is less clear on this point.[65] Kidwai said in 2008 that 'separation is more linked to time rather than space.'[66] In addition to preventing unintentional detonation, separation of the components enhances nuclear safety, physical security and maintenance access. The move toward flexible deterrence with the employment of battlefield-use nuclear weapons may change this.

If trends concerning battlefield nuclear weapons persist, Feroz Khan anticipates that Pakistan will likely shift from a recessed nuclear deployment toward an ambiguous state of deployment by 2015–17.[67] At least one Islamabad editorialist argues that plugging the deterrence gap requires Pakistan to move to a concept of 'ready deterrence'.[68] This would mean having assembled nuclear weapons deployed in a ready-to-use posture.

Such a move toward hair-trigger alert status would increase nuclear dangers in several respects. Fully assembled weapons would be more alluring to terrorists and their transfer from central storage bunkers to missile sites could make them more vulnerable to theft, seizure and insider appropriation. Although safety measures would still be in place to minimise unauthorised use, there is a heightened risk to the safety of weapons that are in deployed status. Most importantly, shortening the alert status dangerously heightens the risk of inadvertent or unauthorised nuclear use and the potential for a nuclear war due to miscalculation and misperception. The history of other nuclear-armed states demonstrates the danger. During the Cold War, the US and USSR came perilously close to nuclear exchange as a result of mistakes and misperceptions on several occasions.[69] Michael Krepon argues that in South Asia 'the probability of first use as a result of accidents and unauthorized use … appears greater than a deliberate command decision to cross the nuclear threshold.'[70]

The circumstances of the India–Pakistan confrontation increase the dangers. Geographic adjacency sharply reduces the warning time, while the deployment of dual-use aircraft and missiles heightens the risk of misperception. Hotlines have gone unused in crisis situations and command-and-control mechanisms are still under development. In the near background lurks the frequency of India–Pakistan warfare and crises. For either country to now adopt a hair-trigger posture could produce extreme instability.[71]

The introduction of TNWs increases the complexity of command-and-control arrangements. Even before *Nasr* came into the picture, Narang described the 'ominous deterrence/management trade-off' that Pakistan faced, or what Scott Sagan terms the 'vulnerability/invulnerability paradox'.[72] To deter a conventional Indian attack, Pakistan believes it must portray a credible willingness to resort first to nuclear weapons. But enhancing credibility can sacrifice central government control over nuclear assets in a crisis situation.[73] This operational dilemma is multiplied by the addition of TNWs, which must be deployed close to the forward edge of battle to be effective.

The other danger of pre-delegation is unauthorised use. As retired Indian Brig. Gurmeet Kanwal put it:

> The command and control of TNWs needs to be decentralised at some point during war to enable their timely employment. Extremely tight control would make their possession redundant and degrade their deterrence value. Decentralised control would run the risk of their premature and even unauthorised use.[74]

One reason why NATO policy planning moved away from the use of TNWs is because the security of the short-range weapons and the maintenance of command and control could not be ensured during war situations.[75]

Feroz Khan wrote in 2005 that 'partial pre-delegation' would be an 'operational necessity because dispersed nuclear forces as well as central command authority ... are vulnerable. Should a trade-off be required, battle-effectiveness of the nuclear force will trump centralized control.'[76] Pakistani security scholar Zafar Nawaz Jaspal contends that, during a crisis, Pakistan's short-range weapons are to be deployed to the battlefield and delegated to the local commander, which could even be an army lieutenant-colonel.[77] Physicist Abdul Hameed Nayyar echoed this belief in a 2013 press interview: 'You are actually delegating responsibility' to commanders at 'very, very low' echelons.[78]

Rejecting such assumptions, the SPD insists that the control of all nuclear weapons will remain centralised under the

National Command Authority (NCA). The short-range nuclear weapons will not be deployed to forward positions, nor will use be delegated to field commanders.[79] The SPD's resistance to calls for pre-deployment of its TNWs is to be applauded on the grounds of nuclear security. The no pre-delegation decision is explained by geographic logic. Because Pakistan's territory is relatively narrow, the TNWs will only have to be moved a short distance to be readied for battlefield use. For strategic use, nuclear weapons might be deployed 200km away from the border. For battlefield use, they might be stationed 60–100km away from the border.[80] The short-range systems reportedly can be moved from storage sites to forward locations within a few hours, not days. Thus, it is claimed that there is no need for pre-delegation of firing authority and therefore no possibility of misuse by a field commander.[81]

Some of the reassuring claims by Pakistan's military are not entirely convincing. According to a 2012 press release, an automated 'Strategic Command and Control Support System' has been established to provide 'round the clock situational awareness' of all strategic assets to central decision-makers.[82] As the United States has found, however, the most robust of command-and-control systems cannot overcome human error. As late as 2007, a US Air Force crew inadvertently transported six nuclear-armed cruise missiles without realising for 36 hours that the weapons were not conventional.[83] Such mishaps are more likely in the fog of war. Retired Pakistan Army Lt.-Gen. Talat Masood recently noted the practicality problem with TNWs: 'If the conditions are unstable, and if you are that close to the border, then you can't really exercise physical control.'[84] Pakistan's ultimate answer to the vulnerability/invulnerability paradox is that the dilemma will be moot because the credibility added to their deterrence posture by the introduction of TNWs will dissuade Indian Army incursions into Pakistani territory.[85]

Nuclearisation of the sea

In theory, the development of sea-based platforms can aid crisis stability if they create a secure second-strike capability. By ensuring the survivability of a portion of the nation's nuclear arsenal, concealable sea-based systems avoid the 'use them or lose them' dilemma that national leaders might otherwise face in a nuclear crisis. The development of sea-based nuclear systems can also be destabilising, however, because it entails more weapons, new types of weapons and more fissile material. In South Asia, the introduction of sea-based systems further stimulates the nuclear arms race, as each party seeks to match the adversary's capabilities. Determined to neutralise the advantage that India has gained in the maritime field with its introduction of both aircraft carriers and nuclear-armed submarines, Pakistan may seek to develop naval tactical nuclear weapons for use against Indian carrier groups.

Sea-based nuclear systems also increase the danger of inadvertent or unauthorised use because it is nearly impossible at sea to keep the warheads and missiles separated. At sea, mated nuclear weapons may be under the control of the ship captain. Technological fixes can minimise, but not eliminate, the risk. Adding to the danger, the maritime environment in South Asia is 'alarmingly unstructured', in the words of military analyst Iskander Rehman. None of the confidence-building measures or conflict-resolution mechanisms that India and Pakistan have adopted to date cover their naval forces. He describes a Pakistani proclivity for naval brinkmanship by threatening to collide with Indian naval ships and buzzing Indian flotillas with maritime aircraft.[86] The introduction of nuclear systems at sea makes such incidents fraught.

The danger is exacerbated by the ambiguity of dual capability inherent in the sea-based systems. The nuclear-capable missiles being developed for the respective navies also can carry conventional arms. As Rehman notes, the blurring of platform and mission categories would add to the fog of war, making it impossible to discriminate between nuclear and conventional attacks.[87]

The destabilising nature of dual-use delivery systems applies equally to land- and sea-based systems, but is most pronounced with cruise missiles, which are nearly undetectable and very difficult to defend against once they are launched. Preparations for the use of dual-use systems can easily be misread as preparations for nuclear use and could spark a pre-emptive attack. Whether based on sea, land or air platforms, cruise missiles can also be destabilising by their capability to evade missile-defence systems. Countering India's fledgling BMD programme is one of Pakistan's incentives for developing nuclear-armed cruise missiles.

Impact on CTBT and FMCT

The nuclear arms competition in South Asia has global repercussions for arms control. It has stymied an international quest for a treaty to stop the production of fissile material for nuclear weapons and cast a shadow on entry-into-force provisions for the Comprehensive Nuclear-Test-Ban Treaty (CTBT). The two treaties are top priorities for global arms control, featuring prominently, for example, in the disarmament agenda US President Barack Obama laid out in Prague in April 2009. The treaties also offer the best hope for controlling the South Asian arms race because treaties with equal international application are more likely to win domestic support than is the case with unilateral pressure tactics.

Efforts to bring about an FMCT accelerated in 1993 when the UN General Assembly adopted a resolution calling for the negotiation of such a treaty. In 1995, the Geneva-based Conference on Disarmament (CD) agreed to establish a committee for this purpose. To date, however, substantive negotiations have yet to begin. One delay was caused by the US administration of George W. Bush, which in 2004 opposed the inclusion of a verification mechanism on the grounds that the treaty could not be effectively verified. Obama reversed the US position in 2009, and the CD in May that year agreed again to establish a negotiating committee. Although Pakistan had gone along with the consensus on that vote, later that year it blocked the CD from implementing the agreed programme of work. The single-handed veto has remained in place ever since, to the annoyance of much of the world, including UN Secretary-General Ban Ki-moon.[88]

Islamabad sees the FMCT as being a Pakistan-specific instrument and justifies its veto on the grounds of the 2008 NSG waiver granted to India on nuclear cooperation and the potential, in theory, that this gives India to use its domestic uranium reserves for warhead production. Only if Pakistan receives a similar exemption from NSG guidelines will it allow FMCT discussions to proceed. But this alone will not turn Pakistan into an FMCT supporter. To join a fissile material cut-off, Pakistan has stated other conditions.

Pakistan believes that treaty conditions banning only future production would lock in India's perceived advantage in fissile-material stockpiles. Pakistan thus insists that, rather than simply a cut-off, a 'fissile material control regime' should also address existing stockpiles by reducing asymmetries. States with the largest stockpiles should cut back their holdings first, with progressive stock reductions to follow for the rest.

Even if all these conditions were met, Pakistan can be expected to find other reasons not to accept an FMCT. Given Pakistan's sense of paranoia about the United States and India having intentions of seizing its warheads, the military leadership is unlikely to accept the intrusive verification measures by international inspectors that would be required to address existing stockpiles. Pakistan is also unlikely to agree to limiting its fissile-material production until it believes it has sufficient stockpiles for a credible deterrence. Nuclear experts at the Carnegie Endowment for International Peace state it bluntly: 'Pakistan's real opposition to an FMCT is the constraints it would place on Pakistan's nuclear modernization.'[89]

The unfortunate irony in this position is that without agreed limits, India is much better placed by means of its larger nuclear infrastructure and economic advantages to rapidly increase its fissile-material stockpile. Today, the stockpiles of fissile material dedicated to weapons use in each country are relatively equal, if one leaves out the plutonium in the spent fuel from India's power reactors. The plutonium in this spent fuel is not well suited for weapons anyway but an FMCT presumably would prevent reprocessing of it for weapons use.

The arms competition has also made Pakistan and India less inclined to join the CTBT. Long-standing efforts to supplement the partial test-ban treaty with a ban on all nuclear-weapons tests came to fruition after the Cold War ended. CTBT negotiations concluded in 1996 and the treaty was adopted by a large majority of the UN General Assembly. After the South Asian nuclear tests in 1998, the Clinton administration sought vigorously to persuade India and Pakistan to sign the treaty. India agreed to accede if other signatories ratified without conditions, and Pakistan pledged that it would sign if India did. The two are among the 44 states that must sign and ratify the treaty before it can enter into force.

Sixteen years later, the number of ratifications required for CTBT entry into force has shrunk to eight. Meanwhile, however, South Asian attitudes toward the treaty have hardened. In 2009, Pakistan's Foreign Ministry spokesman said that circumstances had changed and Pakistan had no plan to sign the CTBT.[90]

It is not inconceivable that Pakistan would determine that cold testing provides sufficient confidence in its weapons designs. Under this scenario, signing the CTBT might be considered an attractive diplomatic bait in exchange for a deal that accorded Pakistan an NSG exemption for nuclear cooperation. If India signs a CTBT first, there will be enormous pressure on Pakistan to follow suit. Common wisdom that Pakistan will follow whatever India does in terms of CTBT signature and ratification is over-simplified, however; Pakistan would likely require a quid pro quo of its own.

NATO analogies

Pakistani strategists see their position as analogous to that of NATO in the early 1950s, when TNWs were introduced to supplement defence against a potential blitzkrieg invasion by Warsaw Pact forces. Like Western Europe then, Pakistan faces a numerically superior enemy army and relies on nuclear weapons to negate its opponent's conventional advantage. SPD officials are well versed in NATO nuclear doctrine and like to quote Quinlan's aphorism that the Alliance's nuclear weapons would be used 'as late as possible and as early as necessary'.[91] NATO's battlefield-use weapons were initially seen as a more credible deterrent than the policy of massive nuclear retaliation against Soviet cities. Like Pakistan today, NATO did not count on these weapons to stop invading Soviet tank formations. By 1968 the purpose of non-strategic nuclear weapons was no longer military but political.[92] They were to act as a tripwire and to send a political signal of Alliance resolve.

The Pakistan–NATO analogy is stretched, however. NATO's reliance on these weapons was temporary; beginning in 1979, they started to be withdrawn in large numbers.[93] Political doubts about using nuclear weapons on the battlefield emerged as war games showed that the resulting radiation would kill large numbers of allied civilians and render huge areas of land unusable. As the dark adage went, 'the shorter the range, the deader the Germans'. The realisation of the potential for widespread collateral damage led to a more nuanced approach, with progressively less delegation to the theatre commander and a change of doctrine to using nuclear weapons only as a last resort.[94] By 1992, the US Army had removed all of its TNWs from Europe, while the US Air Force kept a small number mainly as a political reassurance to allies. The UK and France also gave up TNW capabilities. While nuclear first use was retained as a theoretical option, it lost credibility as a practical policy because of the uncontrollable escalation that would likely ensue.[95]

The lessons that NATO planners drew about TNWs should have resonance in South Asia, where such weapons have been under discussion for only three years. There remains ample time to make course adjustments. The necessary special arrangements for command-and-control, support, operational-security, situational-awareness and force-protection infrastructure for TNWs have yet to be developed in Pakistan.[96] A sufficient appreciation of the implications of TNWs is also lacking. While India and Pakistan will have carried out their own war games about the use of nuclear weapons, the casualty figures are not public knowledge. Indeed, popular discourse about the human and physical cost of nuclear use is far less prevalent than in many other parts of the world. This is particularly the case in Pakistan.

At an academic forum in Islamabad in 2013, the author was shouted down when he raised the grim notion of 'the shorter the range, the deader the Punjabis'. The retort was that the *Nasr* would not be targeted at populated areas inside Pakistan. If India really were to attack with eight integrated battle groups, however, TNWs employed against all of them would devastate swaths of agricultural heartland. The author was also reminded that no Pakistani official has said the weapons would be used on the nation's own soil, even though this is the obvious conclusion to draw from statements about using the 60km-range *Nasr* in case India launches a cross-border offensive.

David Smith, who twice served as US military attaché in Pakistan and who spent much of the rest of his government career as a nuclear analyst, produced a seminar paper in 2013 that explained in overwhelming logic why NATO strategists concluded that TNWs do not belong on the modern battlefield. He gave the following reasons:

- They add little to the deterrence value provided by strategic nuclear weapons.
- They invite pre-emption when any movement of the weapons from non-deployed status is observed.
- They are not effective against tank formations, which move too fast and can be dispersed.
- They complicate command, control and communications to a degree that does not exist in conventional warfare due to aspects such as nuclear safety locks and the need for secure communication channels at a battle time of maximum vulnerability.
- They require time-consuming launch-approval procedures because of the fateful consideration that must be given by the highest-level national authorities.
- They are difficult to secure when deployed and require scarce manpower to guard them around the clock. According to one estimate, 10% of US military manpower in Europe was required for the special protection and handling of the non-strategic nuclear weapons.
- The dual-use systems must be withdrawn from the battlefield to ensure their survivability, leaving fewer conventional assets to employ in battle.[97]

In sum, US and other NATO military officers found TNWs to be a costly encumbrance with little practical utility. They concluded that precision-guided missiles, multiple-launch rocket systems and attack helicopters provided a more effective defence against a limited conventional attack, and had the additional benefit of being usable in other contexts.[98]

In 1991, US President George H.W. Bush and Soviet President Mikhail Gorbachev made reciprocal unilateral decisions to remove from active service all ground-launched short-range nuclear weapons, as well as sea-based tactical nuclear weapons. Over two decades later, these measures remain firmly in place. One hopes that South Asian leaders will consider taking similar visionary steps of their own to reduce the dangers posed by the South Asian nuclear arms race.

Notes

1   Paul Bracken, 'The Problem from Hell: South Asia's Arms Race', *The Diplomat*, 29 November 2012, http://thediplomat.com/2012/11/29/nuclear-south-asia-the-problem-from-hell/.

2   Ira Helfand, 'Nuclear Famine: Two Billion People at Risk? Global Impacts of Limited Nuclear War on Agriculture, Food Supplies and Human Nutrition', International Physicians for the Prevention of Nuclear War, Physicians for Social Responsibility, November 2013, http://www.psr.org/assets/pdfs/two-billion-at-risk.pdf.

3   Discussions in Islamabad, Rawalpindi and New Delhi, 2011 and 2013.

4   Stockholm International Peace Research Institute, *SIPRI Yearbook 2013: Armaments, Disarmament and International Security* (Oxford: Oxford University Press, 2013), http://www.sipri.org/yearbook/ 2013/06.

5   SIPRI's 2013 estimate for India and Pakistan's weapons holdings both increased by ten weapons. In India's case, the increase was not based on an assumption about fissile-material production; rather it reflected the deployment of the *Agni*-II and assumptions about production of warheads for the K-15 submarine-launched ballistic missile (SLBM).

6   Based on an estimated capacity of 15,000 SWU per year, which is to double by 2016. Uranium Enrichment and Fuel Fabrication - Current Issues (Asia), http://www.wise-uranium.org/epasi.html.

7   International Panel on Fissile Material (IPFM), 'Global Fissile

Material Report 2013', p. 13, http://fissilematerials.org/library/gfmr13.pdf.

8   Alexander Glaser and M.V. Ramana, 'Weapon-Grade Plutonium Production Potential in the Indian Prototype Fast Breeder Reactor', *Science & Global Security*, vol. 15, no. 2, 2007, pp. 85–105, http://scienceandglobalsecurity.org/archive/2007/10/weapon-grade_plutonium_product.html.

9   Pallava Bagla, 'The Fast Breeder Programme just cannot be put on the civilian list', *The Indian Express*, 8 February 2006.

10 Shannon N. Kile, Phillip Schell and Hans M. Kristensen, 'World Nuclear Forces', *SIPRI Yearbook 2012: Armaments, Disarmament and International Security* (Oxford: Oxford University Press, 2012); and 'Nuclear Power in India', World Nuclear Association, 10 April 2013.

11 IPFM, 'Global Fissile Material Report 2011', p. 23, http://fissilematerials.org/library/gfmr11.pdf.

12 David Albright and Serena Kelleher-Vergantini, 'Construction Finishing of Likely New Indian Centrifuge Facility at Rare Materials Plant', Institute for Science and International Security, Imagery Brief, 4 December 2013, http://www.isis-online.org/uploads/isis-reports/documents/RMP_4_Dec_2013.pdf.

13 Rajat Pandit, 'PM takes stock of country's nuclear arsenal', *Times of India*, 14 June 2012.

14 Shiv Aroor, 'New chief of India's military research complex reveals brave new mandate', *India Today*, 3 July 2013.

15 Gulshan Luthra, 'DRDO fires on towards MIRV capability', IANS, 11 April 2013, http://in.news.yahoo.com/drdo-fires-towards-mirv-capability-104607314--finance.html.

16 Vivek Raghuvanshi, 'India To Extend Range of Missile Interceptor to 5,000 Km', *Defense News*, 18 June 2013.

17 Vipin Narang, 'Five Myths about India's Nuclear Posture', *The Washington Quarterly*, vol. 36, no. 3, Summer 2013, p. 147.

18 In April 2013, India claimed that the Chinese army had crossed the Line of Actual Control into Arunachal Pradesh 600 times in the past three years. Rajat Pandit, '600 border violations by China along LAC since 2010', *Times of India*, 23 April 2013. No exchanges of fire have been reported, however.

19 S. Paul Kapur, 'India and Pakistan's Unstable Peace', *International Security*, vol. 30, no. 2, Fall 2005, pp. 138–39.

20 Vipin Narang, 'Indian Nuclear Posture: Confusing Signals from DRDO', Institute for Defence Studies and Analyses (IDSA) Comment, 26 September 2011, http://www.idsa.in/idsacomments/IndianNuclearPostureConfusingSignalsfromDRDO_vnarang_260911.

21 'India creates 60 – 170 km Pragati – Tactical Missile', Indian Defence Forum, 26 October 2013, http://defenceforumindia.com/forum/strategic-forces/55359-india-creates-60-170-km-pragati-tactical-missile.html.

22 Zahir Kazmi, 'SRBMs, Deterrence and Regional Stability in South Asia: A Case Study of Nasr and Prahaar',

Institute of Regional Studies, 2012, p. 23.

23 Frank O'Donnell, 'Managing India's Missile Aspirations', IDSA, 10 February 2013, http://idsa.in/idsa comments/ManagingIndiasMissile Aspirations_fodonnell_100213.

24 Vladimir Radyuhin, 'BrahMos Gains Sub-/Strategic Super Weapon Capability', *The Hindu*, 13 October 2012; and Narang, 'Five Myths about India's Nuclear Posture', p. 146.

25 David O. Smith, 'The US Experience with Tactical Nuclear Weapons: Lessons for South Asia', Stimson Center, 4 March 2013, p. 28, http://www.stimson.org/ images/uploads/research-pdfs/ David_Smith_Tactical_Nuclear_ Weapons.pdf. These 11 systems include three variants of the *Prithvi* SRBM with ranges between 150 and 350km; the *Agni*-I SRBM with a 700km range; the *Prahaar* SRBM with a 150km range; the *Dhanush* naval SRBM with a 350km range; two anti-shipping missiles, the 65km *Ametist* and 78km *Popeye*; and three cruise missiles, the 1,000km *Nirbay*, 290km *BrahMos* and 120km *Moskit*.

26 Lt.-Gen. (Retd) Raghavan, Reducing Nuclear Risks in South Asia', Stimson Center, Washington DC, 18 October 2012, http://www.stimson. org/images/uploads/research-pdfs/ Reducing_Nuclear_Risks_in_ South_Asia_-_Raghavan.pdf.

27 Gurmeet Kanwal, 'Does India Need Tactical Nuclear Weapons?', IDSA, New Delhi, May 2003, http://www. idsa-india.org/an-may-03.html.

28 Manoj Joshi, 'Ballistic Missile Nasr—A Bigger threat from

Pakistan', *India Today*, 2 June 2011; and Brahma Chellaney, 'Nuclear Deterrent Posture', in Brahma Chellaney (ed.), *Securing India's Future in the New Millennium* (New Delhi: Orient Longman Limited, 1999), pp. 209–14.

29 Shashank Joshi, 'India's Military Instrument: A Doctrine Stillborn', *Journal of Strategic Studies*, vol. 36, no. 4, May 2013, p. 517.

30 South Asian Strategy Stability Institute, 'Workshop on Indian Military's Cold Start Doctrine and its Implications for Strategic Stability in South Asia', 20–22 July 2010, http://www.sassu.org.uk/ pdfs/Cold%20Start%20Workshop. pdf.

31 Author discussion with Pakistani scholar, December 2012.

32 'No Cold Start Doctrine, India Tells US', *The Indian Express*, 9 September 2010.

33 Walter C. Ladwig, 'A Cold Start for Hot Wars? The Indian Army's New Limited War Doctrine', *International Security*, vol. 32, no. 3, 1 January 2008, p. 176.

34 Anit Mukherjee, 'The absent dialogue', *Seminar*, July 2009, www. india-seminar.com/2009/599/599_ anit_mukherjee.htm.

35 Joshi, 'India's Military Instrument', p. 521.

36 Manoj Joshi, 'Who is afraid of Cold Start? Certainly not Pakistan', *Mail Today*, 17 February 2010, http:// mjoshi.blogspot.co.uk/2010/02/ who-is-afraid-of-cold-start-certainly.html.

37 IISS–CISS seminar in Islamabad, 10 December 2013.

38 'Indian Military Rehearse Pakistan's Dissection in Mock Battles', Agence

France-Presse, 3 May 2006, cited in H. Nayyar and Zia Mian, 'The Limited Military Utility of Pakistan's Battlefield Use of Nuclear Weapons in Response to Large Scale Indian Conventional Attack', Pakistan Security Research Unit, Brief Number 61, 11 November 2010, p. 3, http://www.princeton.edu/sgs/faculty-staff/zia-mian/Limited-Military-Utility-of-Pakistans.pdf.

39 'Army Able To Launch Faster Response Against Pakistan', Business Standard, 13 January 2012.

40 Smith, 'The US Experience with Tactical Nuclear Weapons', p. 32.

41 Tariq Osman Hyder, 'Strategic restraint in South Asia', Nation, 20 March 2013.

42 'Ballistic missile defence key area for India-US ties: Carter', New York Daily News, 23 July 2012.

43 Peter R. Lavoy, 'Islamabad's Nuclear Posture: Its Premises and Implementation', in Henry D. Sokolski (ed.), Pakistan's Nuclear Future: Worries Beyond War (Carlisle, PA: Strategic Studies Institute, 2008), p. 156.

44 Paul Kerr, 'U.S. Nuclear Cooperation with India: Issues for Congress', Congressional Research Service (CRS), 26 June 2012, p. 8, http://www.fas.org/sgp/crs/nuke/RL33016.pdf. Kerr cites a memorandum from Air Commodore Khalid Banuri, SPD Director of Arms Control and Disarmament Affairs, received by CRS analyst, 4 December 2011.

45 Smith, 'The US Experience with Tactical Nuclear Weapons', p. 32.

46 Tahir Khan, 'Pakistan concerned at Indian ballistic missile system', News Pakistan, 9 May 2013, http://www.newspakistan.pk/2013/05/09/pakistan-concerned-indian-ballistic-missile-system/.

47 Usman Ansari, 'Pakistan Seeks to Counter Indian ABM Defenses', Defense News, 21 March 2011; and Zahir Kazmi, 'Weapons of Peace', The Express Tribune, 26 June 2012, http://tribune.com.pk/story/399425/weapons-of-peace/?print=true.

48 Kazmi, 'SRBMs, Deterrence and Regional Stability in South Asia', p. 14.

49 Robert Jervis, The Illogic of American Nuclear Strategy (Ithaca, NY: Cornell University Press, 1984), pp. 148–49.

50 Rodney Jones, 'Pakistan's Answer to Cold Start', Friday Times, 13–19 May 2011, http://www.thefridaytimes.com/13052011/page7.shtml.

51 Paul Kapur, 'Stability and Deterrence in South Asia', talk at the National Defense University, 14 March 2013.

52 Adil Sultan, 'Pakistan's emerging nuclear posture: impact of drivers and technology on nuclear doctrine', Institute of Strategic Studies Islamabad, 17 April 2012, pp. 160–61, http://www.issi.org.pk/publication-files/1340000409_86108059.pdf.

53 'Missile technology: Pakistan tests nuclear-capable Hatf IX', Agence France-Presse, 30 May 2012.

54 Michael Quinlan, Thinking About Nuclear Weapons: Principles, Problems, Prospects (New York: Oxford University Press, 2009), p. 21.

55 Sultan, 'Pakistan's emerging nuclear posture', p. 154.

56 Kazmi, 'SRBMs, Deterrence and Regional Stability in South Asia', p. 25.

57 Michael Krepon, 'Brodie's Weakest Book', Arms Control

Wonk, 17 September 2012, http://krepon.armscontrolwonk.com/archive/3540/brodies-weakest-book.

58 Gurmeet Kanwal, 'Tactical Nuclear Weapons: Pakistan Playing a Dangerous Game', *Tribune*, 16 October 2012.

59 Shyam Saran, 'Is India's Nuclear Deterrent Credible?', speech at India Habitat Centre, New Delhi, 24 April 2013, http://krepon.armscontrolwonk.com/files/2013/05/Final-Is-Indias-Nuclear-Deterrent-Credible-rev1-2-1-3.pdf.

60 Indrani Bagchi, 'Strike by even a midge nuke will invite massive response, India warns Pak', *Times of India*, 30 April 2013.

61 IISS–CISS workshop in Islamabad, November 2013. Some Indian scholars also question the credibility. See Rajesh Rajagopalan, 'India's Doctrinal Options', in Gurmeet Kanwal and Monika Chansoria (eds), *Pakistan's Tactical Nuclear Weapons: Conflict Redux* (New Delhi: KW Publishers, 2013), pp. 208–09.

62 Rajaram Nagappa, Arun Vishwanathan and Aditi Malhotra, 'HATF-IX/NASR – Pakistan's Tactical Nuclear Weapon: Implications for Indo-Pak Deterrence', National Institute of Advanced Studies, Bangalore, India, July 2013, p. 33, http://isssp.in/wp-content/uploads/2013/07/R17-2013_NASR_Final.pdf.

63 Then-President Musharraf said in 2003 that the missiles and warheads are stored separately. See 'No Possibility of Nuke War: Musharraf', Rediff.com, www.rediff.com/news/2003/jan/10pak1.htm, 10 January 2003. Several official and unofficial non-Pakistani sources have corroborated this statement. Christopher Clary, 'Thinking about Pakistan's Nuclear Security in Peacetime, Crisis and War', IDSA, Occasional Paper No. 12, September 2010, p. 10, http://www.idsa.in/system/files/OP_PakistansNuclearSecurity.pdf.

64 Ashley Tellis, *India's Emerging Nuclear Posture: Between Recessed Deterrent and Ready Arsenal* (Santa Monica, CA: RAND, 2001), p. 367, http://www.rand.org/content/dam/rand/pubs/monograph_reports/2008/MR1127part1.pdf. For a more recent, contrary assessment, see Narang, 'Five Myths about India's Nuclear Posture', pp. 148–50.

65 IISS, *Nuclear Black Markets: Pakistan, A.Q. Khan and the rise of proliferation networks – A net assessment* (London: IISS, 2007), p. 33. A CRS report notes that there is contradictory evidence about whether Pakistan has in fact kept its weapons de-mated. Paul Kerr and Mary Beth Nikitin, 'Pakistan's Nuclear Weapons: Proliferation and Security Issues', CRS, 13 February 2013, http://www.fas.org/sgp/crs/nuke/RL34248.pdf, p. 15. See also Bruno Tertrais, 'Pakistan's nuclear programme: a net assessment', Fondation pour la Recherche Stratégique, 13 June 2012, p. 9, http://www.frstrategie.org/barreFRS/publications/rd/2012/RD_201204.pdf.

66 Maurizio Martellini, 'Security and Safety Issues about the Nuclear Complex: Pakistan's Standpoints', Landau Network–Centro Volta, 2008.

67 Feroz Khan, 'Prospects for Indian and Pakistani Arms Control' in Henry Sokolski (ed.), *The Next Arms Race* (Carlisle, PA: Strategic Studies Institute, 2012), pp. 357–84, http://www.npolicy.org/userfiles/image/ub1113.pdf.

68 Zia Siddiqui, 'Ready deterrence vs Recessed deterrence', *News International*, 8 July 2013; Zia Siddiqui, 'Why "Ready Deterrence" for Pakistan?', *News International*, 31 July 2013.

69 Scott Sagan, *The Limits of Safety: Organizations, Accidents, and Nuclear Weapons* (Princeton, NJ: Princeton University Press, 1995). The most dangerous episodes came during the Cuban Missile Crisis in October 1962 and the November 1983 *Able Archer* NATO command-post exercise.

70 Michael Krepon, 'Pakistan's Nuclear Strategy and Deterrence Stability', Stimson Center, 10 December 2012, p. 13, http://www.stimson.org/images/uploads/research-pdfs/Krepon_-_Pakistan_Nuclear_Strategy_and_Deterrence_Stability.pdf.

71 Vipin Narang, 'Posturing for Peace? Pakistan's Nuclear Postures and South Asian Stability', *International Security*, vol. 34, no. 3, Winter 2009/2010, p. 74.

72 Ibid.; and Scott Sagan (ed.), *Inside Nuclear South Asia* (Stanford, CA: Stanford University Press, 2009), pp. 15–16.

73 Narang, *'Posturing for Peace?'*.

74 Gurmeet Kanwal, 'Tactical Nuclear Weapons: Pakistan Playing a Dangerous Game', *The Tribune*, 16 October 2012.

75 Michael Krepon, 'Nuclear Weapons Competition', *Dawn*, 1 January 2013.

76 Feroz Hassan Khan, 'Nuclear Command and Control in South Asia During Peace, Crisis and War', *Contemporary South Asia*, vol. 14, no. 2, June 2005, pp. 168–69.

77 Zafar Nawaz Jaspal, 'Tactical Nuclear Weapon: Deterrence Stability between I dau Network–Centro Volta, ndia and Pakistan', in Feroz H. Khan and Nick M. Masellis, *US-Pakistan Strategic Partnership* (Monterey, CA: Center for Contemporary Conflict, US Naval Postgraduate School, January 2012), http://www.nps.edu/Academics/Centers/CCC/PASCC/Publications/2012/2012_002_Jaspal.pdf.

78 Elaine M. Grossman, 'Pakistan's Military Sanguine on Avoiding Wartime Nuclear Calamity', Global Security Newswire, 3 April 2013, http://www.nti.rsvp1.com/gsn/article/pakistani-military-sanguine-about-avoiding-nuclear-calamity/?mgh=http%3A%2F%2Fwww.nti.org&mgf=1.

79 Krepon, 'Pakistan's Nuclear Strategy and Deterrence Stability', p. 20.

80 Interview with Pakistani scholar, September 2012.

81 Adil Sultan, 'South Asian Stability-Instability Paradox: An Alternate Perspective', unpublished paper, 2013, p. 16.

82 Inter Services Public Relations, Press Release, 17 September 2012, http://www.ispr.gov.pk/front/main.asp?o=t-press_release&date=2012/9/17.

83 Joby Warrick and Walter Pincus, 'Missteps in the Bunker', *Washington Post*, 23 September 2007.

84 Grossman, 'Pakistan's Military Sanguine on Avoiding Wartime Nuclear Calamity'.

85 Krepon, 'Pakistan's Nuclear Strategy and Deterrence Stability', p. 21.

86 Iskander Rehman, 'Drowning Stability: the Perils of Naval Nuclearization and Brinkmanship in the Indian Ocean', *Naval War College Review*, vol. 65, no. 4, Autumn 2012, p. 78, http://www.usnwc.edu/getattachment/187a93e1-db4c-474e-9be8-038bb7a64edb/Drowning-Stability--The-Perils-of-Naval-Nucleariza.aspx.

87 *Ibid.*, p. 82.

88 'UN's nuclear disarmament conference may sink over Pakistan's reluctance: Ban-ki Moon', *Express Tribune*, 25 January 2012.

89 Toby Dalton, Mark Hibbs and George Perkovich, 'A Criteria-Based Approach to Nuclear Cooperation with Pakistan', Carnegie Endowment for International Peace, 22 June 2011, http://carnegieendowment.org/files/nsg_criteria.pdf.

90 'Pakistan Rules Out Test Ban Treaty Endorsement', Global Security Newswire, June 19, 2009, http://www.nti.org/gsn/article/pakistan-rules-out-test-ban-treaty-endorsement/.

91 Quinlan, *Thinking About Nuclear Weapons*, p. 40.

92 Smith, 'The US Experience with Tactical Nuclear Weapons', p. 18.

93 Shashank Joshi, 'Pakistan's Tactical Nuclear Nightmare: Déjà Vu?', *The Washington Quarterly*, vol. 36, no. 3, Summer 2013, p. 166.

94 IISS, 'South Asia's Nuclear Arms Race: Lessons of the Cold War', in *Strategic Survey 2013: The Annual Review of World Affairs* (Abingdon: Routledge for IISS, 2013), p. 38.

95 *Ibid.*, pp. 38–39.

96 *Ibid.*, p. 39.

97 Smith, 'The US Experience with Tactical Nuclear Weapons', pp. 22–27.

98 IISS, 'South Asia's Nuclear Arms Race'.

CHAPTER FOUR

The potential for nuclear terrorism

There is no doubting the potential for nuclear terrorism in Pakistan. Given the large number of radicalised groups, their ruthlessness and brazenness in attacking military targets and the growing size of the nuclear-weapons establishment, the potential intersection of these trends is clear. A congressionally mandated US report in 2008 on preventing proliferation of weapons of mass destruction put it graphically: 'Were one to map terrorism and weapons of mass destruction today, all roads would intersect in Pakistan.'[1] The creeping fundamentalism throughout Pakistani society sparks an additional concern about insider collusion that might enable terrorists to evade security measures. However, much of the Western discourse about these concerns is exaggerated. The threat is typically hyped and the efforts that Pakistan has taken to reduce the risks too often overlooked. As described in this chapter, while it may be true that no country is more likely than Pakistan to spawn nuclear terrorism, it is probably also true that no country has done more to secure its nuclear infrastructure.

Defining nuclear terrorism

Nuclear terrorism can appear in various ways.[2] The most terrifying scenario is the acquisition – by theft, purchase or other insider collusion – of a nuclear weapon. Detonation of the weapon could kill 100,000 people or more. Suicide-minded terrorists would not need missiles or aircraft to deliver the weapon; it could be transported by truck or boat. This nightmare scenario may be the least likely means of nuclear terrorism, however, given the control exerted over nuclear arsenals and the methods used to prevent their unauthorised misfiring. A higher probability scenario, albeit one that is still unlikely, would involve the acquisition of fissile material by terrorists with the right nuclear engineering background to be able to fabricate and detonate a crude nuclear weapon. Building a modern nuclear implosion device is probably beyond the capabilities of any non-state actor,[3] but not so an improvised gun-type nuclear bomb. A US government study in 1977 concluded that a small group of people could possibly design and build a crude nuclear explosive device using 'only modest machine-shop facilities', if they obtained sufficient fissile material.[4] Compared to complete nuclear weapons, fissile material may be under less strict security control, particularly when it is being moved through the various stages of bomb fabrication. Given Pakistan's porous borders, any fissile material stolen there could easily be smuggled elsewhere.

A third potential form of nuclear terrorism involves sabotage or an attack on a nuclear facility. Under certain circumstances, sabotage of a nuclear power plant could produce a disaster on the scale of Chernobyl or Fukushima. The devastation from such an attack would be akin not to a nuclear weapon with its potent blast and heat effects, but to a large dirty bomb that spews poisonous radiation. As in Fukushima, the resultant death count would be low but the environmental and economic costs could be massive.

For the purposes of this book, nuclear terrorism is considered to fall into one of the above three scenarios. There is, however, a fourth type of nuclear terrorism: detonation of an actual dirty bomb, using radioactive sources, such as cobalt-60, strontium-90, caesium-137 or iridium-192, which are used in industrial and medical applications. Although dirty-bomb scenarios entail less physical damage, they are more likely to be employed, given the thousands of radiological sources used throughout the world and the simplicity of making radiological-dispersion and radiological-emission devices. The risk of a radiological attack is not necessarily greater for Pakistan than for other countries. Pakistan has adopted the International Atomic Energy Agency (IAEA) Code of Conduct on the Safety and Security of Sealed Radioactive Sources and the Pakistan Nuclear Regulatory Authority tracks the radioactive sources that are imported into the country. Reports that al-Qaeda in 2003 was making a dirty bomb in Afghanistan, from which it might have sought to transport it to Pakistan,[5] have never been confirmed.

Presence of terrorist groups

The warnings about nuclear terrorism in Pakistan stem mainly from the growth of terrorism itself in that nation. Pakistan has been called the epicentre of global Islamic jihad[6] and parts of the country have been a safe haven for al-Qaeda and other terrorist groups. Although the circumstances of Osama bin Laden's last years – living in the shadow of the military academy at Abbottabad – were shocking, it was no surprise that he found sanctuary in Pakistan. So, too, with principal architect of the 9/11 attacks Khalid Sheik Mohammed, before his capture, in March 2003, by the CIA and Pakistan's Inter-

Services Intelligence (ISI) agency. As of end-2013, three of the world's most-wanted terrorists were believed to be living in Pakistan: Hafiz Muhammad Saeed (Lashkar-e-Taiba, LeT), Ayman al-Zawahiri (al-Qaeda) and Mullah Mohammad Omar (Afghan Taliban).

After years of Pakistan's leadership soft-pedalling the home-grown terrorism problem, in a speech on Independence Day in August 2012, Chief of Army Staff General Pervez Kayani condemned extremism and terrorism, which he said could lead Pakistan to civil war, and called for mobilisation of the entire nation against terrorism.[7] Essays published by the Pakistani military in a so-called 'green book' describe home-grown militant groups as the biggest threat to the nation's security. Media reports incorrectly described the essays as representing a shift in the military's doctrine,[8] but they do represent an acknowledgment of the problem. The frequency and ferocity of terrorist attacks on government forces led Khawaja Khalid Farooq, the former head of Pakistan's National Counter Terrorism Authority, to say in July 2013 that the country was 'bleeding'.[9] As of April 2013, 5,000 Pakistani soldiers and 17,000 civilians had lost their lives since the United States launched its so-called 'war on terror' in 2001. Terrorists groups operating in the country are estimated to number from 30 to up to 60.[10]

Documents seized in the raid on bin Laden's compound indicated that al-Qaeda had a larger presence in Pakistan than was previously thought. The US government had estimated the group to number 300–400 in Pakistan. But just one 'company' identified in the documents as being led by Badr Mansoor, who was killed by a US drone attack in February 2012, had more than 2,200 members, including 350 hard-core fighters and more than 150 suicide bombers.[11] Another al-Qaeda unit in Pakistan, Brigade 313, is reportedly as large as the Badr Mansoor group. The Qari Zafar group is estimated to number in the thousands, if supporters as well as fighters are included,[12] although none of these numbers are confirmed. Al-Qaeda is affiliated with several other terrorist groups in Pakistan including Jaish-e-Mohammed (JeM), LeT, Harkat-ul-Jihad-al-Islami and Lashkar-e-Jhangvi.[13]

Many of the terrorist groups are part of a loose umbrella organisation called Tehrik-e-Taliban Pakistan (TTP), formed in the aftermath of the government's July 2007 counterproductive attack on militants holed up in the Red Mosque. American terrorism expert Charles Blair calls these actors the 'Pakistani Neo-Taliban'. In his words, it is 'clearly the greatest non-state threat to Pakistan's overall security and, more specifically, its nuclear assets' because of the group's unique combination of ideology, strategic objectives, organisational structure, relations with other groups, connections with elements of the Pakistani state, and overall resources and capabilities.[14] One expert estimates that the TTP has access to tens of millions of dollars and has 20,000 or more fighters. In addition to carrying out targeted acts of terrorism, the TTP operates both as an effective army and as an insurgency movement. It also has access to massive amounts of weapons and military-grade explosives.[15]

Major operations have included an 11 March 2008 attack on the Federal Investigation Agency in Lahore by a truck bomb that killed 30 people; a 20 September 2008 truck bomb attack on the Marriott Hotel in Islamabad that killed 62 people; a January 2009 attack on a paramilitary Frontier Corps base in Mohmand district that involved hundreds of fighters armed with machine guns and rocket-propelled grenades; a 3 March 2009 commando-style ambush of the Sri Lankan cricket team in Lahore which used anti-tank missiles; a 27 May 2009 attack on ISI Provisional Headquarters in Lahore, killing 29; a 13 April 2012 attack against the central jail in the northwestern city of Bannu by 200 heavily armed TTP militants; and a 31 July 2013 attack on another northwestern jail, this time in Dera Ismail Khan, both of which freed hundreds of jihadist inmates.

Terrorists have also conducted brazen attacks against military bases. On 1 November 2007, a suicide bomber attacked a bus at Sargodha air base in Punjab, resulting in 11 deaths, including seven officers. On 10 December 2010, a suicide bomber attacked an air-force school bus outside the gate of the aerospace complex at Minhas air base at Kamra in Punjab, injuring seven. On 21 August 2008, two TTP militants conducted a suicide attack at the gate of the ordnance factories at the military city of Wah, killing 70 workers. On 10 October 2009, terrorists using automatic weapons, grenades and rocket launchers attacked the army's General Headquarters in Rawalpindi, holding 42 hostages for 18 hours and killing a brigadier-general among other casualties. On 23 May 2011, 15–20 heavily armed jihadists penetrated the outer perimeter of the Mehran naval air base near Karachi and engaged security forces in a firefight that lasted several hours and destroyed several aircraft. On 16 August 2012, nine TTP fighters penetrated the Minhas air base, killing two officials and destroying one aeroplane.

The extent to which terrorism affects Pakistan is summed up in the US State Department's 2012 annual terrorism report:

> Over 2,000 Pakistani civilians and 680 security forces personnel were killed in terrorist-related incidents in 2012. Terrorist incidents occurred in every province. Terrorists attacked Pakistani military units, police stations, and border checkpoints, and conducted coordinated attacks against two major military installations. Terrorists displayed videos on the internet of the murders and beheadings of security forces. Terrorist groups also targeted police and security officials with suicide bombings and improvised explosive

devices (IEDs). Terrorist groups targeted and assassinated tribal elders, members of peace committees, and
anti-Taliban government officials.[16]

In contrast to al-Qaeda and TTP, which target the Pakistani
state, LeT primarily operates against India and is thus seen
by many countrymen as 'good' jihadists.[17] As mentioned in
Chapter Two, LeT was responsible for both the 2001 raid on
the Indian parliament and the 2008 Mumbai massacre. Over
the years, LeT has received extensive support from the ISI to
conduct operations in Kashmir. Whether this support continues today is debatable. LeT now has independent financial
resources from its extensive system of charities and other
social services as well as organised crime.[18] LeT oversees
terrorist training camps that have produced between 100,000
and 300,000 fighters over the past two decades.[19] Leaders of
the group have gone so far as to call for nuclear jihad against
India. In January 2011, LeT leader Saeed said it would be 'no
problem' if fighting over Kashmir led to nuclear war between
Pakistan and India.[20]

A nuclear terrorism fact sheet published by Harvard
University's Belfer Center website in 2010 lists LeT as among
four terrorist groups that 'have demonstrated interest in acquiring a nuclear weapon'.[21] Terrorism expert Rolf Mowatt-Larssen,
who spent most of his career in the US intelligence community
and is now at the Belfer Center, wrote in 2010 that LeT was
among the groups that 'have manifested some degree of intent,
experimentation, and programmatic efforts to acquire nuclear,
biological and chemical weapons'. There is no further substan-
tiation in the public realm. When asked, he judged that the
LeT's interest in such weapons is more opportunistic than
systematics and more inclined toward radiological terrorism
than nuclear weapons.[22]

Terrorist interest in nuclear weapons

Notwithstanding the difficulty in sourcing the LeT's alleged interest in nuclear weapons, the intersection between Pakistan's nuclear programme and the terrorist groups on its territory is visible in other ways, including at least two cases of Pakistani nuclear scientists discussing nuclear technology with terrorist groups.

Al-Qaeda's interest in nuclear weapons, going back to the mid-1990s, is well documented.[23] In 1998, Osama bin Laden declared that acquiring weapons of mass destruction for the defence of Muslims is a religious duty. In his 1998 treatise, *The Exoneration*, Zawahiri justified use of weapons of mass destruction on religious grounds. In October 2001, shortly after the 11 September terrorist attacks on the World Trade Center and the Pentagon, US intelligence agencies learnt that retired Pakistani nuclear scientists Sultan Bashirudin Mahmood and Abdul Majid had been meeting with al-Qaeda leaders in Afghanistan that summer. Mahmood, who had been demoted at the Pakistan Atomic Energy Commission (PAEC) for supporting militant Islamic groups, founded a charity relief agency called Ummah Tameer-e-Nau (UTN, meaning, roughly, 'Islamic revival'), which he used as a front to help the Taliban in Afghanistan. UTN was well established among Pakistan's elite; its membership included General Hamid Gul after he retired as head of ISI. When later interrogated, Mahmood and Majid claimed that their meetings in Afghanistan with the Taliban had been sanctioned by the intelligence agency.[24]

In several meetings with bin Laden, Zawahiri and other members of al-Qaeda, Mahmood and Majid discussed nuclear-weapons technology. When interrogated by ISI, Mahmood said he had explained to bin Laden the difficulty of constructing a uranium-enrichment facility, and that bin Laden then asked him, 'what if you already have the enriched uranium?'[25]

Mahmood, who had made speeches saying that Pakistan's nuclear capability was the property of the global Muslim community, drew rough diagrams of nuclear-weapon designs for bin Laden. Neither he nor Majid were weapons experts, however, so they could not have taught al-Qaeda how to build the weapons. Al-Qaeda also asked them for help with making radiological dispersal devices, though it is not clear if work on a dirty bomb went beyond an agreement in principle.[26]

Al-Qaeda was not UTN's only nuclear connection. According to the head of Libyan intelligence Musa Kousa, UTN had approached Libya to offer help in building a nuclear bomb.[27] And UTN was not al-Qaeda's only connection to the Pakistani nuclear programme. Several other Pakistani nuclear scientists were reportedly contacted by the Taliban and al-Qaeda for cooperation in establishing a nuclear-weapons project in Afghanistan.[28] When the CIA sought to interview two of them, Suleiman Asad and Mohammed Ali Mukhtar, Pakistani authorities reportedly said they were unavailable because they had been sent to Myanmar on a research project.[29]

In June 2009, Mustafa Abu al-Yazid, the leader of al-Qaeda in Afghanistan, told Al Jazeera, 'God willing, [Pakistan's] nuclear weapons will not fall into the hands of the Americans and the mujahedeen would take them and use them against the Americans.'[30] The next month Zawahiri appealed to Muslims at Pakistan's nuclear facilities to consider their loyalties, claiming that the US intended to seize Pakistan's nuclear weapons and implying that they should instead help al-Qaeda gain access to the arsenal.[31]

Leaders of other terrorist groups in Pakistan have echoed this theme. A 12 March 2012 video communiqué by Omar Khalid, emir of the Mohmand tribal agency, affiliated with the TTP, spoke of the need to ensure that Pakistan's nuclear weapons should be used to safeguard the interests of the umma, the greater Muslim community, and not serve American interests. Some Western analysts interpreted the video as Khalid calling for TTP to seize and use the nuclear weapons. This questionable interpretation is inconsistent with the TTP's previously stated position. In 2008, TTP chief Baitullah Mehsud told Al Jazeera that the TTP was not thinking of using nuclear weapons because they kill innocent women and children, which is forbidden in Islam.[32] In May 2011, the group's main spokesman, Ehsanullah Ehsan, insisted that the TPP had no plan whatsoever to attack Pakistan's nuclear assets.[33]

One year later, however, the ISI reportedly intercepted a telephone communication in which the TTP spoke about finalising plans for attacking the uranium conversion facility at Dera Ghazi Khan. The planned attack was said to be in revenge for the killing of the head of their group in south Punjab. In reaction to the intercept, the army and police deployed a large number of forces near the nuclear installation.[34]

The Hizb ut-Tahrir (HuT) has also advocated that Pakistan's nuclear arsenal be put at the disposal of the wider umma. Founded in Jordan in the early 1950s, HuT, which describes itself as a political party but is accused of working with al-Qaeda, focused its activity in Pakistan after the 1998 tests. According to its manifesto, HuT seeks to establish a caliphate super-state based in the Saudi peninsula, formed of Muslim majority countries, and sees Pakistan's nuclear technology as useful to this endeavour.[35] The group's Pakistan branch issued a statement in 2008 calling on the Pakistani military to use nuclear weapons against the United States.[36] The HuT does not conduct acts of terrorism in Pakistan, but is often seen as the most insidious of the jihadist groups because of its recruitment efforts within the officer corps and among well-educated professionals.

However one interprets the nuclear intentions of Pakistani terrorist groups, it should be noted that none of the aforementioned attacks on military facilities have been directed against the nuclear arsenal. Some descriptions miss this nuance. British South Asian expert Shaun Gregory, for example, mischaracterised the suicide attack against a bus outside Sargodha air base as being an attack 'at the missile storage facility' of the air base, and called the December 2007 suicide attack on a school bus outside Minhas air base an attack on 'Pakistan's nuclear airbase'.[37] It might also be noted that none of the documents seized from Osama bin Laden's home in Abbottabad or on his computers showed any interest in Pakistan's nuclear weapons.[38]

While some of Gregory's examples are exaggerated, his larger point should not be dismissed. Terrorists brazen enough to attack army headquarters and well-connected enough to know where jihadist suspects were being detained at Mehran naval air base[39] may employ similar tactics to try to break into nuclear-weapons storage facilities.[40] Chances of such success at nuclear facilities are far lower, however, because of extensive security measures employed to protect what are the nation's most prized possessions.

Western assessments

However reassuring those physical protection measures may be, the United States gives intense emphasis to the security of Pakistan's nuclear programme. A summary of the US intelligence community's confidential budget, leaked in September 2013, described ramped-up intelligence of Pakistan's nuclear arsenal. As reported by the *Washington Post*, 'fears about the security of its nuclear program are so pervasive that a budget section on containing the spread of illicit weapons divides the world into two categories: Pakistan and everybody else.' The document warned that 'knowledge of the security of Pakistan's nuclear weapons and associated material encompassed one of the most critical set of … intelligence gaps.' Those blind spots

were especially worrisome, it said, 'given the political instability, terrorist threat and expanding inventory [of nuclear
weapons] in that country'.[41] Attesting to the intelligence gap,
former chairman of the US National Intelligence Council
Thomas Fingar said in 2011: 'We do not know if what the military has done is adequate to protect the weapons from insider
threats, or if key military units have been penetrated by extremists. We hope the weapons are safe, but we may be whistling
past the graveyard.'[42]

Qualitative and quantitative changes in Pakistan's nuclear-
weapons programme exacerbate Western concerns. US officials
have voiced their worries directly to Pakistan, warning that the
move to tactical nuclear weapons (TNWs) creates a greater risk
of theft or diversion.[43] So too, the larger number of weapons
and the larger number of facilities. Doubling the number of
plutonium-production reactors does not double the risk, since
all are co-located, but the increased risk is not miniscule. Each
new facility requires additional technicians, managers and
security personnel, any one of whom could present an internal
security risk.

In the Western think-tank community, Pakistan's reputation
has generally fared poorly, with greater attention to the dangers
and less to Pakistan's efforts to overcome the dangers. This is
partly due to confidentiality; many of the steps Pakistan has
taken are not put before the public in any detail and those that
are disclosed are typically not confirmable. In January 2012, the
Washington-based Nuclear Threat Initiative (NTI) published
its first Nuclear Materials Security Index, benchmarking
nuclear-materials security conditions on a country-by-country
basis. Of 32 countries that have 1kg or more of weapons-usable
nuclear materials, Pakistan was ranked 31st, above only North
Korea, with below-average scores in the categories of sites
and transportation; political stability; 'group(s) interested in

illicitly acquiring materials'; 'material production/elimination trends'; pervasiveness of corruption; and physical security during transport.[44] Pakistan scored above average in terms of how well it implements its international legal obligations but it did not score as high as it could have due to a lack of publicly accessible information about security and control measures.[45] When NTI updated the index in January 2014, Pakistan was lauded for having undertaken the most improvements to its nuclear-security regulations and practices, and it was ranked 22nd among 25 countries with weapons-usable nuclear materials.[46]

Nuclear-security measures

In response to the leak of the intelligence budget, which came at the hands of fugitive intelligence contractor Edward Snowden, the US State Department spokesperson offered reassurance:

> The United States is confident that the Government of Pakistan is well aware of its responsibilities and has secured its nuclear arsenal accordingly. While there is room for improvement in the security of any country's nuclear programs, Pakistan has a professional and dedicated security force that fully understands the importance of nuclear security.[47]

Responsibility for protecting Pakistan's strategic programmes against both inside and outsider threats is entrusted to the Strategic Plans Division (SPD). For the past 14 years the SPD was under the command of General Kidwai, who continued to serve for over six years after his formal retirement from the military in 2007. Contrary to the usual promotion and retirement norms of the Pakistan Army, many of his deputies also retained their positions year after year. This longevity in position provided a sense of stability for Pakistan and reassurance to its foreign partners, who uniformly praised Kidwai's leadership and the SPD's integrity and competence. On the other hand, in a country of weak institutions where patronage and personality-dominated politics trump organisational bonds, there was some risk in relying so exclusively on one man's leadership. His replacement, Lt.-Gen. Zubair Mahmood Hayat, took over in March 2014.

SPD officials describe a four-tier approach to ensuring nuclear security, including physical protection, human reliability programmes, an emergency management system and comprehensive training. For physical protection, the SPD's Security Division employs a force of 20,000 personnel, up from 12,000 at the beginning of the decade, to independently secure the nuclear facilities. There is now a Special Response Force, a Site Response Force and a Marine Response Force. These SPD forces are supplemented by regular air defence and infantry elements of the Pakistan Army. The multi-layered defence is supplemented by modern surveillance and detection equipment, including infrared and motion sensors, video cameras and communications devices.[48] Satellite imagery shows that security at certain nuclear facilities has been increased in recent years, with wider security perimeters around all four reactor facilities at Khushab.[49] A system of sensitive material control and accounting is in place involving regular and surprise inspections and an inventory system to track individual components of warheads. Kidwai's claim that all fissile material is accountable 'down to the last gram',[50] is exaggerated; every nuclear facility in the world has a certain amount of 'material unaccounted for' because of uranium stuck in the piping, for example, but the intention to employ strict accountability deserves recognition. For storage and transport, tamper- and theft-proof containers are employed. The security perimeter is enhanced at a third level by counter-intelligence teams that identify and assess threats. Other security measures to protect the arsenal against seizure include phony bunkers and dummy warheads and the policy of de-mating warheads from missiles or bomb casings.

At the second tier, personnel reliability programmes based on robust recruitment, extensive vetting and personnel minding are designed to ensure 'workplace trustworthiness' – namely loyalty and mental balance. Exceeding international best practices, workers are monitored before, during and after employment, with clearance rechecks every two years.[51] The screening assesses psychological and medical health, political affiliation, financial background and religious beliefs. The screening programme is administered by the SPD in cooperation with Pakistan's three intelligence agencies: the ISI, Military Intelligence and the Intelligence Bureau. The scale of A.Q. Khan's proliferation activity clarified the need for such personnel vetting. Monitoring during retirement was added after retired PAEC officials were discovered to have met with al-Qaeda leaders. It is questionable, however, whether close tabs can be kept on all the workers employed in Pakistan's nuclear programme, including after retirement. The workforce in the nuclear programme is thought to number between 40,000 and 70,000.[52] Greatest attention, naturally, is given to the 2,000 scientists and engineers working in particularly sensitive areas or possessing critical knowledge.[53]

Thirdly, a Nuclear Emergency Management System is coordinated through a round-the-clock Nuclear and Radiological Emergency Support Centre. Fourthly, and most recently, comprehensive training is provided by a specialised training academy in all aspects of nuclear safety and security disciplines. Pakistan has offered the training academy as a centre of excellence for regional and international cooperation on nuclear security through the IAEA. This state-of-the-art facility in Kallar Kahar is comparable to the US Department of Energy's academy in Albuquerque, New Mexico.[54]

The offer of the training academy as a regional centre of excellence was a Pakistani contribution to the 2012 Nuclear Security Summit in Seoul. In its national progress report at the Seoul Summit, Pakistan also tallied other steps it had taken to improve export controls, secure radiological sources and prevent nuclear smuggling. Under its renewed Nuclear Security Action Plan, first established in 2006, Pakistan is upgrading the physical security at its 11 nuclear medical centres, which use radioactive sources that could be used in a dirty bomb.[55] One indication of the respect the international community has for Islamabad's efforts to enhance nuclear security is that Pakistan was among ten nations asked to play a key role in the Sherpa process in the run-up to the 2012 summit, by leading the discussion on coordination of existing initiatives.

Other ways in which Pakistan contributes to international efforts to enhance nuclear security include its active participation in the Global Initiative to Combat Nuclear Terrorism and the US-led Container Security Initiative. In addition, Pakistan in 2004, 2005 and 2008 submitted reports to the UN committee overseeing implementation of UN Security Council Resolution 1540. The reports detail steps Pakistan has taken to implement the resolution, which mandates states to criminalise the proliferation of weapons of mass destruction and their means of delivery and requires states to adopt strict export controls. Pakistan has also acceded to the Convention on the Physical Protection of Nuclear Material but, like the majority of states, not yet its 2005 amendment, which would extend protection requirements to apply to nuclear facilities and materials in peaceful domestic use and storage. Pakistan is also not yet party to the International Convention for the Suppression of

Acts of Nuclear Terrorism, which as of February 2014 had 91 parties.

Pakistan's nuclear-security measures were significantly enhanced by a nuclear command-and-control mechanism that was instituted in 2000. This set up the National Command Authority (NCA) with operational control of all nuclear assets, from research and development to employment. The ten members include the president, prime minister, ministers of foreign affairs, defence, interior, chairman of the Joint Chiefs of Staff Committee, the chiefs of army, navy and air force, and the director general of the SPD, which acts as the secretary of the authority. Although the prime minister nominally chairs the NCA, in practice the military is in charge. Reporting to the NCA are Strategic Forces Commands in each of the services which exercise technical, training and administrative control over the strategic delivery systems, while authority to launch rests with the NCA. No single individual can issue a launch order and a standard 'two-man rule' is employed to authenticate access to nuclear release codes.

Among other measures, Pakistan has developed its own version of 'permissive action links' (PALs), the sophisticated locks designed to prevent accidental or unauthorised launching of nuclear weapons. The US is prevented by the Nuclear Non-Proliferation Treaty (NPT) and its export-control laws from providing modern PAL technology and Pakistan is wary of accepting technology that might include 'kill switches' that might enable the US to disable the weapons. Pakistan thus developed its own PAL system, composed of a 12-digit alphanumeric code. Until the code is released by the NCA, the warheads are effectively duds. Some experts are not convinced, however, that Pakistan's PALs measure up to international standards. One reason for scepticism goes back to the command-and-control conundrum of how Pakistan will ensure that weapons which are kept de-mated and in central storage during times of peace will be usable in time of need.

Pervez Hoodbhoy argues that Pakistan's 'compulsion to protect its nuclear weapons by dispersing them and to keep them usable could require loosing central authority to such an extent that PALs would be effectively neutralised as a crisis threatened to turn into war'.[56] He also notes that it is not possible to verify the applicability of the two-man rule.[57] Vipin Narang agrees that 'Pak-PALS' are likely weak, bypassable controls that allow for rapid release of nuclear weapons if deemed necessary.[58] Since Western PALs are digitally integrated into fully assembled nuclear weapons, he argues that a PAL for de-mated Pakistan nuclear weapons would not meet international standards. US nuclear expert Jeffrey Lewis similarly argues that Pak-PALS likely are not PALS per se, but rather 'coded-control devices that allow the arming of a nuclear weapon from either the cockpit of an aircraft or a missile launcher … Such use-control devices are an important safeguard, but codes … can be exposed and external devices bypassed.'[59]

Security controls can be circumvented, often by design for deterrence purposes.[60] At times of crisis, the PAL access codes might be provided to commanders for fear of a breakdown in communications that would render the weapons useless. Feroz Khan writes that the 'theater commander would probably take matters into his own hands … Should a trade-off be required, battle effectiveness of the nuclear force will trump centralized control.'[61] This impulse is not unique to Pakistani commanders. 'Unlock codes' for American intercontinental ballistic missiles (ICBMs) reportedly were routinely set to 00000000 for much of the Cold War.[62] The insistence by Pakistani authorities that there will be no pre-delegation of authority would be sorely tested in a conflict scenario.

In contrast to more developed countries, which emphasise technological solutions to nuclear security, Pakistan relies on the human factor: large numbers of security forces to protect against outsider threats and intrusive vetting, policing and counter-intelligence to protect against insider threats. Given the chaotic state of the nation's electrical grid, not relying on technology makes sense. On the other hand, the degree of corruption, cronyism and incompetence found throughout the country[63] and the creeping fundamentalist bent of elements of Pakistani society cannot help but raise questions about the reliability of security programmes focused on personnel. The competence of the Pakistani military came into question, for example, when US Navy SEALs were able to get past air defences, land helicopters close to the military academy, kill bin Laden and get away before authorities were any the wiser.[64]

Embarrassing as the bin Laden snatch was to the Pakistani military as a whole, the lapses in that case should not impinge on the reputation of the SPD. Pakistan's air-defence forces should have been alert to American helicopters, but they were not charged with protecting bin Laden. The SPD forces have the exclusive mission of protecting the nation's most precious assets, and they are widely regarded as fit for purpose. Shashindra Tyagi, a former chief of staff of the Indian Air Force, acknowledged their competence: 'The Pakistani military understands the [nuclear security] threats they face better than anyone, and they are smart enough to take care [of] it.'[65]

Many of the improvements in Pakistan's nuclear command and control over the past decade were undertaken with US assistance. Since September 2001, the US has provided about US$100 million to Pakistan in the form of nuclear-security training, technical support and equipment.[66] Pakistan now has in place a strict system of accounting for sensitive material production, verified by surprise inspections. There is probably little more that the US could do to help Pakistan improve its nuclear security except through ongoing training assistance and the provision of the newest portal monitors that detect intrusions and other such equipment.

Paranoia about the US

Humiliation over the bin Laden snatch has fed paranoia in Pakistan that the United States is bent on seizing Pakistan's nuclear weapons. As expressed in a *New Yorker* article, 'Fear of pernicious American designs on Pakistan's nuclear arsenal has combined with people's anger over their military's apparent impotence, creating a feeling of almost toxic insecurity across the country.'[67] Still seething about the breach of Pakistani sovereignty two weeks afterwards, General Kayani sought to obtain a written guarantee from visiting Senate Foreign Relations Committee Chairman John Kerry that US forces under no circumstances would enter Pakistan to try to seize or secure the nuclear arsenal. As a legislator, Kerry had no authority to sign such a statement, but did declare that the United States has no designs on Pakistan's weapons.[68]

It is true, of course, that Washington opposed Pakistan going nuclear and the fear of Pakistani nuclear weapons coming under control of extremists remains a top US priority. However, the suspicion that US forces would therefore try to seize the arsenal pre-emptively is far-fetched. Bin Laden was a single, virtually unguarded target. Pakistan's nuclear weapons are disbursed in perhaps 10–15 strongly defended bunkers and are moved from time to time. Even in the unlikely event that the US knew where the weapons were at any given time, it would not be possible, short of a full-fledged invasion, to overcome the multiple layers of security forces and seize the weapons. The US is not a threat to Pakistan's arsenal; it wants only to help Pakistani authorities keep their nuclear assets secure.

The only eventuality in which the US would consider trying to secure one or more of Pakistan's nuclear weapons would be in the event that they otherwise were about to fall into terrorist hands, such as in the case of a collapse of the state and of the army. For years the US Joint Special Operations Command (JSOC), an elite counter-terrorism force, has trained for the mission of securing and neutralising nuclear weapons anywhere in the world where they might be under threat of acquisition by terrorist groups.[69] Journalistic accounts of JSOC forces actively preparing missions into Pakistan have been highly exaggerated, however.[70]

It is popularly reported that many of the nuclear-security measures taken by Pakistan are designed not for protection against terrorists or insider threats but rather to protect the weapons against seizure by the US or India.[71] After both the 11 September 2001 terrorist attacks in the US and the May 2011 Abbottabad raid, Rawalpindi reportedly redeployed its nuclear arsenal.[72] Some critics also believe that Pakistan's move toward smaller, and more, nuclear weapons was motivated by the fear of a US raid, on grounds that redundancy in numbers makes it harder to seize them all.[73] Such reasoning would make for a vicious cycle: the more weapons, the greater the US concern, which when communicated to Pakistan feeds paranoia about ulterior US motives and the perceived need for yet more redundancy and mobility of weapons thus more susceptibility to their loss to terrorists. The underlying assumption is weak, however. As discussed in Chapter Three, Pakistan's motivations for more and different kinds of nuclear weapons are predominantly India-centric. There is no denying the concern about US intentions and Pakistan's response in terms of moving and hiding the weapons. But there is no evidence that such concerns affect nuclear-posture planning and Pakistani authorities refute the claim.[74] It should also be noted that since late 2012, relations with the United States have improved after two highly contentious years.[75]

Potential for insider collusion

What many see as a growing fundamentalist bent of Pakistani society stokes concerns about the potential for insider collusion with violent jihadists in acquiring nuclear assets or sabotaging nuclear facilities. Prominent Pakistani security analyst Imtiaz Gul recently warned that many low-ranking security officials have sympathies for the Taliban and other militant groups and that this could pose a 'real threat' to the nation.[76] Hoodbhoy writes of a 'heavily Islamicized rank and file brimming with seditious thoughts'.[77] When Zawahiri and Omar Khalid called for Pakistan's nuclear assets to be put to the use of the umma, they were effectively seeking to induce collaboration from such sympathisers. Specific concerns have been raised about jihadist sympathies in the ISI, given the connections the ISI has developed with such groups and the agency's increased role in protecting the nuclear arsenal. Christopher Clary recommends that any ISI official involved in such protection duties should be subject to the same scrutiny about personnel reliability accorded to others in the nuclear establishment.[78]

The involvement of security personnel in high-level assassination cases has raised doubts about the effectiveness of Pakistan's reliability screening. Lower-ranking air-force officers were reportedly involved in assassination attempts against President Musharraf in 2006 and 2009. It should be noted, however, that the officers had not gone through any special security screening.[79] More worrisome was the January 2011 assassination of Punjab governor Salman Taseer by a member of his own security detail, supplied by the elite force of the provincial police. The killer's motive was Taseer's opposition to Pakistan's blasphemy law. He had called for the release of a

Christian woman who was condemned to death for allegedly making derogatory remarks about the Prophet Muhammad. The killer fired 27 shots without interference by other security guards. The fact that his act was applauded not only by 500 conservative religious scholars but also by hundreds of Pakistani lawyers is an indication of the growing radicalisation of civil society. The judge who sentenced the assassin had to flee the country because of death threats and Taseer's son was abducted in August 2011 and has not been heard from since.

Mowatt-Larssen writes that 'nowhere in the world is this [insider] threat greater than in Pakistan,' and notes the nation's 'dismal track record in thwarting insider threats'. The nuclear-related examples he cites – A.Q. Khan's exports and UTN's conversations with al-Qaeda – are those that sparked the state to reform the way the nuclear programme is controlled and monitored.[80] Other cases of terrorist attacks for which there have been allegations of insider collusion, such as the March 2009 attack on the Sri Lankan cricket team, the May 2012 jail break in Bannu and the attacks on ISI headquarters, had nothing to do with the nuclear programme.

This does not mean, of course, that there are no insider threats in the nuclear establishment. In 2009, an unnamed US official expressed concern about what he saw as 'steadfast efforts of different extremist groups to infiltrate the labs and put sleepers and so on in there'.[81] In a February 2009 cable that was made public by WikiLeaks, the US Embassy in Islamabad warned about the potential for insider collusion in obtaining weapons-usable fissile material: 'Our major concern is not having an Islamic militant steal an entire weapon but rather the chance someone working in GOP [government of Pakistan] facilities could gradually smuggle enough material out to eventually make a weapon.'[82] Harvard nuclear security expert Matthew Bunn agrees that the greatest concern is insider theft of fissile material, noting that this was the case in all but one of the reported instances of highly enriched uranium (HEU) and plutonium smuggling globally.[83]

While the scenario of small-scale diversion via insider collusion cannot be dismissed, it should be recognised that most reported global cases of nuclear-materials smuggling involve large-scale plants in the former Soviet Union that have been operating for decades and where there is a sizeable surplus stockpile. Fissile-material production in Pakistan takes place at a smaller scale and with greater strategic need for strict accounting.

Transport vulnerability

As in most countries, Pakistan's nuclear assets are probably most vulnerable while nuclear material and warheads are being transported from one secure facility to another. Separated plutonium and HEU must be moved from Islamabad and Kahuta – 60km and 80km away respectively – to the pit fabrication and warhead assembly facilities, presumably both at the Wah munitions complex. The warheads must then be transported to their storage sites at Fatehjang, Sargodha, Shanka Dara, Quetta and elsewhere.[84] Occasionally they must be moved back to Wah for maintenance and refurbishment. Warheads are also moved from site to site as a precaution against pre-emptive attack and seizure. Some components of the weapons are transported by helicopter but much of the transport is by road. Non-state actors would find it harder to plan an attack on a mobile nuclear unit than one at a fixed site, but the difficulty could be overcome if the group was able to acquire insider information about movements.

Pakistan's road network is congested, substandard and dangerous. Accidents present the main danger, but terrorist attacks are not unheard of. In 2008, Lieutenant-General

Mushtaq Ahmed Baig, Pakistan's surgeon general, was assassinated by a suicide bomber while he was stopped at a traffic light on his way home from work.[85] Most of the nuclear-weapons facilities are located in the northern and western parts of the country, near areas where the TTP is most active.[86]

The SPD understands the transportation vulnerability problem and has taken steps to address it, including by giving police and civilian security personnel training in nuclear security. In the civilian nuclear-security sector, spent fuel is kept at the nuclear power plants at Karachi and Chashma, with no plans to move it elsewhere for storage. The Pakistan Nuclear Regulatory Authority adheres to a Nuclear Security Action Plan for handling nuclear material and follows IAEA physical protection standards. But as noted above, Pakistan has not yet ratified the 2005 amendment to the Convention on the Physical Protection of Nuclear Material which applies standards to domestic transportation of nuclear material.

Another measure the SPD has taken to address transportation vulnerability is controversial, at least as seen by foreign observers. To mask transit of sensitive nuclear materials and warheads, Pakistan transports them clandestinely, reportedly in unmarked vehicles rather than heavily armed visible convoys.[87] Given the domestic threat environment, this is reasonable; movements of nuclear material should not be done in an obvious manner. Yet the reduced security presence for such movements increases the risk of an attack by terrorists with foreknowledge of the transport. The possibility that extremists have infiltrated security forces and know when and where nuclear warheads are being transported cannot be discounted. Another potential downside to disguised transport of sensitive assets is the possibility of inadvertent assault by militants or common criminals not knowing what is being carried by anonymous-looking vehicles.

Transport vulnerability will be higher during times of crisis with India, when launchers and warheads may be moved from fixed locations to avoid pre-emptive attacks. The command-and-control difficulty discussed in Chapter Three also impacts nuclear security. Nuclear forces will naturally be placed on higher alert during a crisis, and as the crisis escalates, security procedures are likely to be stressed, making the weapons more vulnerable to theft, accident or unauthorised use.

Comparison with India and other countries

For all the attention focused on the risk of nuclear terrorism in Pakistan, the potential risk may be greater in India. In terms of both competence and commitment to nuclear security, Western officials judge Pakistan to be well ahead of its rival.[88] In contrast to the intense focus the SPD gives to nuclear security and the assistance it receives from the US in this regard, Indian attitudes are sometimes described in terms of near nonchalance. This may reflect a relative lack of knowledge of Indian nuclear-security practices in the military field. Clary comments that 'it is possible the world knows less about India's nuclear weapons program than any other nuclear state except North Korea.' It is not known if India employs permissive action links and, if so, how robust and tamper-resistant they are.[89] Narang draws similar conclusions: 'There is almost no public assessment or discussion about the threats to the security of India's civilian and military nuclear assets, and how robust India's security measures are against those threats.'[90]

If any of Pakistan's extremist groups sought to employ nuclear terrorism, they are more likely to do so against India. It stands to reason that violent jihadists would want radiological damage visited not upon lands of the umma but against the enemy infidel. David Headley, the US-born LeT accomplice implicated in the 2008 Mumbai attack, reportedly carried out surveillance on the Bhabha Atomic Research Centre in Trombay, Mumbai. In August 2012, India arrested 18 people said to be connected with Pakistani terrorist groups who were reportedly planning attacks on the Kaiga nuclear power plant and other facilities.[91] A year later, India captured the head of Indian Mujahideen, Ahmad Zarar Siddibapa, who reportedly confessed that he had sought to acquire a 'small nuclear device' from Pakistan to detonate in Surat, India. In response to his request, his Pakistan-based boss allegedly told him that 'anything can be arranged in Pakistan.'[92] Such fanciful plans are far easier said than carried out, of course.

In assessing nuclear vulnerabilities in South Asia, it is also fair to note the nuclear-security lapses that have occurred in other countries. Over the years, there has been an appalling number of instances in the United States, for example, of careless handling of nuclear weapons, including the 2007 case of a US Air Force crew transporting six nuclear weapons, believing them to be conventional warheads. In 2012, three peace activists, including an 82-year-old nun, broke into the Y-12 National Security Complex in Oakridge, Tennessee, where they splashed human blood on the uranium storage site. Security tests performed at other nuclear-weapons related sites the next year uncovered one worrisome scenario in which mock commandos gained access to simulated bomb material.[93] Peace activists have also broken into a presumed nuclear-weapons storage site in Belgium, a nuclear power plant in Sweden and several French nuclear facilities. More worrisome than these symbolic intrusions was the 2007 armed break-in at South Africa's Pelindaba nuclear facility, where 600kg of HEU is stored. Two other security violations occurred at Pelindaba in 2005 and 2012.[94]

Assessment

The nightmare scenario of Pakistan's nuclear weapons falling into terrorist hands via a fundamentalist takeover of the state cannot be dismissed as hostile Western propaganda. Egyptian Mohamed ElBaradei, former head of the IAEA, is among those who have expressed the same fear.[95] Former prime minister Benazir Bhutto herself said in 2007 that the army's control over the nuclear arsenal could weaken due to instability in the country.[96] In response, SPD officials point out that Islamist groups cannot come to power through democratic means because of their low level of popular support. Nor, Kidwai says, can they overthrow a military as cohesive, disciplined and middle-class oriented as the Pakistani army.[97] Election results bear out the first point; fundamentalist parties have never polled more than 11%. And although public-opinion polls show that most Pakistanis identify more with their religion than their state, they also profess strong faith in the army, which is the only institution in Pakistan that is accorded widespread trust.[98] The strength and integrity of the army is why most analysts familiar with Pakistan agree that there is very little possibility of an Islamist coup.[99] Bruce Riedel offers a dissenting voice: 'The possibility is now real that we will see a jihadist state emerge in Pakistan – not an inevitable outcome, not even the most likely, but a real possibility … And that is the real strategic nightmare for the United States.'[100] As Clary notes, however, neither Riedel nor anybody else has provided a convincing narrative for how radicals could actually take over the country.[101]

As noted, six terrorist attacks have occurred at or near military bases in Pakistan that have been associated with nuclear materials. In none of these cases, however, were nuclear weapons or nuclear material at serious risk of theft by non-state actors with malevolent intentions. The supposed presence of

nuclear weapons appears in every case to have been coinciden-
tal to the motives of the attackers. The terrorist attacks against
military bases have been symbolic in nature, designed not to
seize facilities but to make a statement, and the attackers have
rarely penetrated beyond the perimeter of the base. Although
the security situation in some areas, such as Karachi, is deteriorating, in others, such as the Swat Valley which was overrun by
jihadists in 2007–09, it has improved.

Even if the intention of extremists was to seize nuclear
weapons, they would have to overcome multiple obstacles.
Bruno Tertrais sums up the challenge:

> An attack against a nuclear base would need to
> confound SPD and ISI surveillance, then break the
> physical and military barriers that would preclude
> access to a nuclear weapon. Insider complicity would
> have to defeat the reliability programs. Military
> involvement inside or outside would need a break-
> down in the culture of loyalty inherent to the Pakistani
> armed forces.[102]

The distinction in Pakistan is the worrisome presence of
jihadist groups with malevolent intent and growing capabilities. One senior American official summed up his government's
assessment of Pakistan's nuclear-security profile in this way:
no country pays more attention to nuclear security than
Pakistan; however, this does not make Pakistan's nuclear
assets the most secure, because no country has a greater terrorism problem.[103]

Pakistan must guard against complacency. In putting the
best image forward to the world, Pakistani officials often over-
state the case, in ways that undermine credibility. The Foreign
Ministry typically claims, for example, that the nation's nuclear

assets are 100% secure. In June 2011, Interior Minister Rehman Malik doubled this reassurance, declaring the weapons to be '200 percent safe'.[104] The more realistic narrative is that Pakistan's nuclear weapons are 'at least as safe and secure as those of any other nuclear country'.[105] The SPD certainly understands the threat and is taking steps to address it. But unfortunately, the trend lines of two key factors are moving in ways that exacerbate the concern. The growing extremism and instability of Pakistani society and the growing amount of nuclear material and weapons inevitably cast more focus on Pakistan as the potential epicentre of nuclear terrorism. It is doubly disconcerting that at least some Pakistani officials see the threat to their nuclear assets as coming more from the US than from jihadist groups.

Notes

1 Bob Graham et al., *World at Risk: The Report of the Commission on the Prevention of Weapons of Mass Destruction Proliferation and Terrorism* (New York: Vintage Books, 2008), p. xxiii.

2 This paragraph and the next two draw from Charles D. Ferguson and William C. Potter, 'The Four Faces of Nuclear Terrorism', Center for Nonproliferation Studies, 2004, http://jeffreyfields.net/427/Site/Blog/30F67A03-182C-4FC7-9EFD-A7C321F6DC8D_files/analysis_4faces.pdf.

3 Robin M. Frost, *Nuclear Terrorism after 9/11*, Adelphi Paper 378 (Abingdon: Routledge for IISS, 2006).

4 US Congress, Office of Technology Assessment, 'Nuclear Proliferation and Safeguards', June 1977, p. 140, http://www.princeton.edu/~ota/disk3/1977/7705/7705.PDF.

5 Frank Gardner, 'Al-Qaeda "was making dirty bomb"', BBC News, 31 January 2003, http://news.bbc.co.uk/1/hi/uk/2711645.stm.

6 'Hope is not policy', interview with Bruce Riedel, German Council on Foreign Relations, IP Journal, 12 May 2011, https://ip-journal.dgap.org/en/ip-journal/regions/hope-not-policy.

7 Frederic Grare, 'Is Pakistan's Behavior Changing?', Carnegie Endowment for International Peace, 30 January 2013, http://carnegieendowment.org/2013/01/30/is-pakistan-s-behavior-changing/f76i#.

8 Christine Fair, 'Pakistan Civil War?', *Huffington Post*, 7 January 2013, http://live.huffingtonpost.

com/r/segment/pakistan-defines-its/50e716ce78c90a7ec70002a0.

9 '"Pakistan is bleeding" - ex counter terrorism chief', BBC News, 9 July 2013, http://www.bbc.co.uk/news/world-23242399.

10 Up to 30, according to Brian Cloughley, 'Fission Fears', *Jane's Intelligence Review*, April 2011; up to 50–60, according to David O. Smith, 'The US Experience with Tactical Nuclear Weapons: Lessons for South Asia', Stimson Center, 4 March 2013, http://www.stimson.org/images/uploads/research-pdfs/David_Smith_Tactical_Nuclear_Weapons.pdf.

11 Bill Roggio, 'Bin Laden docs hint at large al Qaeda presence in Pakistan', *Long War Journal*, 9 May 2012, http://www.longwarjournal.org/archives/2012/05/bin_laden_docs_hint.php. Zahir Shah, 'Badr Mansoor, al-Qaeda commander in Pakistan, reported killed', Central Asia Online, 9 February 2012, http://centralasiaonline.com/en_GB/articles/caii/features/pakistan/main/2012/02/09/feature-02.

12 Roggio, 'Bin Laden docs hint at large al Qaeda presence in Pakistan'.

13 *Ibid.*

14 Charles Blair, 'Anatomizing Non-State threats to Pakistan's Nuclear Infrastructure: The Pakistani Neo-Taliban', Federation of American Scientists, Terrorism Analysis Report No. 1, June 2011, http://www.fas.org/pubs/_docs/Terrorism_Analysis_Report_1-lowres.pdf, p. 11.

15 *Ibid.*, pp. 120, 124, 127.

16 Country Reports: South and Central Asia Overview, in 'Country Reports on Terrorism 2012', US State Department, 30 May 2013, http://www.state.gov/j/ct/rls/crt/2012/.

17 'Lashkar-e-Taiba Surpasses al-Qaeda as the Biggest Terrorist Threat from South Asia, Says TRAC', PRWeb, 16 October 2012, http://www.prweb.com/releases/2012/10/prweb10015059.htm.

18 Ashley Tellis, 'The menace that is Lashkar-e-Taiba', Policy Outlook, Carnegie Endowment for International Peace, 13 March 2012, http://carnegieendowment.org/2012/03/13/menace-that-is-lashkar-e-taiba.

19 Mariam Abou Zahab and Olivier Roy, *Islamist Networks: The Afghan-Pakistan Connection* (London: Hurst, 2002), p. 39.

20 'Would not mind Indo-Pak N-war: JuD Chief', Zee News, 6 February 2011, http://zeenews.india.com/news/south-asia/would-not-mind-indo-pak-n-war-jud-chief_685470.html.

21 Graham Allison, 'Nuclear Terrorism Fact Sheet', Policy Memo, Belfer Center for Science and International Affairs, Harvard Kennedy School, April 2010, http://belfercenter.ksg.harvard.edu/publication/20057/nuclear_terrorism_fact_sheet.html.

22 Communication, January 2014.

23 Rolf Mowatt-Larssen, 'Al Qaeda Weapons of Mass Destruction Threat: Hype or Reality?', Belfer Center for Science and International Affairs, Harvard Kennedy School, January 2010, http://belfercenter.ksg.harvard.edu/files/al-qaeda-wmd-threat.pdf.

24 David Albright, *Peddling Peril: How the Secret Nuclear Trade Arms America's Enemies* (New York: Free Press, 2010), p. 178.

25 Ron Suskind, *The One Percent Doctrine: Deep Inside America's Pursuit of Its Enemies since 9/11* (New York: Simon and Schuster, 2006), p. 70.

26 Albright, *Peddling Peril*, p. 179.

27 Suskind, *The One Percent Doctrine*, p. 47.

28 Jack Kelly, 'Terrorists Courted Nuclear Scientists', *USA Today*, 15 November 2001.

29 David Sanger, Douglas Frantz and James Risen, 'Nuclear Experts in Pakistan May Have Links to Al Qaeda', *New York Times*, 9 December 2001.

30 Inal Ersan, 'Al Qaeda says would use Pakistani nuclear weapons', Reuters, 22 June 2009, http://in.reuters.com/article/2009/06/21/idINIndia-40495320090621.

31 Rolf Mowatt-Larssen, 'Islam and the Bomb: Religious Justification for and against Nuclear Weapons', Belfer Center for Science and International Affairs, Harvard Kennedy School, January 2011.

32 Summarised in 'Baitullah Mehsud –Interview', Raman's Pashtun Belt Database blog, 29 January 2008, http://ramanspashtunbeltdatabase.blogspot.co.uk/2008/01/baitullah-mehsud-interview.html.

33 Matthew Rosenberg and Owais Tohid, 'Taliban Say They Won't Hit Nuclear Arsenal', *Wall Street Journal*, 26 May 2011.

34 Abdul Manan, 'Taliban threat: Nuclear site in DG Khan cordoned off', *Express Tribune*, 6 September 2012; and Asad Kharal, 'TTP Punjab rehearsed attack on nuclear site: Report', *Express Tribune*, 7 September 2012.

35 Amir Mir, 'The real face of Hizbul Tehrir', *Asia Times Online*, 28 June 2011, http://www.atimes.com/atimes/South_Asia/MF28Df04.html.

36 'It's America, not Pakistan, that is not in a position to fight another open war', Hizb ut-Tahrir Pakistan Press Statement, 13 September 2008.

37 Shaun Gregory, 'The Terrorist Threat to Pakistan's Nuclear Weapons', *CTC Sentinel*, vol. 2, no. 7, 2009, http://www.ctc.usma.edu/wp-content/uploads/2010/07/CTCSentinel-Vol2Iss7.pdf.

38 Discussion with Western government official, November 2013.

39 Syed Saleem Shahzad, 'Al-Qaeda had warned of Pakistan strike', *Asia Times*, 27 May 2011, http://www.atimes.com/atimes/South_Asia/ME27Df06.html.

40 Shaun Gregory, 'Terrorist Tactics in Pakistan Threaten Nuclear Weapons Safety', *CTC Sentinel*, June 2011, vol. 4, no. 6, pp. 4–7, http://www.ctc.usma.edu/posts/terrorist-tactics-in-pakistan-threaten-nuclear-weapons-safety.

41 Greg Miller, Craig Whitlock and Barton Gellman, 'Top-secret U.S. intelligence files show new levels of distrust of Pakistan', *Washington Post*, 3 September 2013.

42 Jeffrey Goldberg and Marc Ambinder, 'Nuclear Negligence', *National Journal*, 4 November 2011.

43 Eric Schmitt and David E. Sanger, 'In Sign of Normalization, Pentagon to Reimburse Pakistan $688 Million', *New York Times*, 17 December 2012.

44 'NTI Nuclear Materials Security Index: Building a Framework for Assurance, Accountability, and Action', Nuclear Threat Initiative, January 2012, http://www.nti.org/media/pdfs/NTI_Index_FINAL.pdf?_=1326237145.

45 *Ibid.*, p. 29.
46 'NTI Nuclear Materials Security Index: Building a Framework for Assurance, Accountability, and Action – second edition', Nuclear Threat Initiative, January 2014, http://ntiindex.org/wp-content/uploads/2014/01/2014-NTI-Index-Report1.pdf.
47 Jen Psaki, 'Pakistan Nuclear Security', Press Statement, 4 September 2013, US Department of State, http://www.state.gov/r/pa/prs/ps/2013/09/213797.htm.
48 Feroz H. Khan, *Eating Grass: The Making of the Pakistani Bomb* (Stanford, CA: Stanford University Press, 2012), pp. 374–75.
49 David Albright and Robert Avagyan, 'Construction Progressing Rapidly on the Fourth Heavy Water Reactor at the Khushab Nuclear Site', Institute for Science and International Security, 21 May 2012, http://isis-online.org/isis-reports/detail/construction-progressing-rapidly-on-the-fourth-heavy-water-reactor-at-the-k/.
50 Ron Moreau, 'Pakistan Insists Nukes are Safe', *Newsweek*, 25 January 2008.
51 Peter Wonacott, 'Inside Pakistan's Drive to Guard its A-Bombs', *Wall Street Journal*, 29 November 2007.
52 Gregory, 'The Terrorist Threat to Nuclear Weapons in Pakistan'.
53 Bruno Tertrais, 'Pakistan's nuclear programme: a net assessment', Fondation pour la Recherche Stratégique, 13 June 2012, pp. 17–18.
54 Naeem Salik and Kenneth N. Luongo, 'Challenges for Pakistan's Nuclear Security', *Arms Control Today*, March 2013, http://armscontrol.org/act/2013_03/Challenges-for-Pakistans-Nuclear-Security.
55 *Ibid.*
56 Pervez Hoodbhoy, 'Post bin Laden: the safety and security of Pakistan's nuclear arsenal', in Pervez Hoodbhoy (ed.), *Confronting the Bomb: Pakistani and Indian Scientists Speak Out* (Karachi: Oxford University Press, 2013), p. 194.
57 *Ibid.*, p. 192.
58 Vipin Narang, 'Posturing for Peace? Pakistan's Nuclear Postures and South Asian Stability', *International Security*, vol. 34, no. 3, Winter 2009/2010, p. 69.
59 Jeffrey Lewis, 'Managing the Dangers from Pakistan's Nuclear Stockpile', New America Foundation, November 2010, http://newamerica.net/sites/newamerica.net/files/policydocs/111010lewis_paknukes.pdf.
60 Narang, 'Posturing for Peace?', p. 68.
61 Feroz Hassan Khan, 'Nuclear command-and-control in South Asia during peace, crisis and war', *Contemporary South Asia*, vol. 14, no. 2, June 2005, p. 169.
62 Bruce Blair, 'Keeping Presidents in the Nuclear Dark', CDI, 11 February 2004, cited in Lewis, 'Managing the Danger from Pakistan's Nuclear Stockpile', p. 5.
63 Hoodbhoy, 'Post bin Laden', p. 193.
64 Goldberg and Ambinder, 'Nuclear Negligence'.
65 Tom Hundley, 'Pakistan and India: Race to the End', Pulitzer Center, 5 September 2012, http://pulitzercenter.org/reporting/pakistan-nuclear-weapons-battlefield-india-arms-race-energy-cold-war.

66 David Sanger and William Broad, 'U.S. Secretly Aids Pakistan in Guarding Nuclear Arms', *New York Times*, 18 November 2007. Although Pakistani officials dispute this figure, it is consistent with the breakdown of various forms of US assistance to Pakistan that from 2001 to 2012 totalled US$25.9bn. Of that amount, US$115m was provided under 'Non-proliferation, Anti terrorism, Demining and Related' assistance. See 'Direct Overt U.S. Aid Appropriations for and Military Reimbursements to Pakistan, FY2002–FY2014', Congressional Research Service, 11 April 2013, http://www.fas.org/sgp/crs/row/pakaid.pdf.

67 Goldberg and Ambinder, 'Nuclear Negligence'. Such fears are not unprecedented. In late 1979 Pakistan was rife with rumours of an impending US strike against the nation's nuclear installations. When Israel bombed Iraq's Osirak reactor in 1981, many Pakistanis feared that their reactors would be next. See Feroz Hassan Khan, 'Political Transitions and Nuclear Management in Pakistan', in Henry D. Sokolski and Bruno Tertrais (eds), *Nuclear Weapons Security Crises: What does history teach?* (Carlisle, PA: Strategic Studies Institute and US Army War College Press, 2013), p. 159.

68 David E. Sanger, *Confront and Conceal: Obama's Secret Wars and Surprising Use of American Power* (New York: Broadway Books, 2012), p. 109.

69 Seymour M. Hersh, 'Watching the Warheads: The Risks to Pakistan's Nuclear Arsenal', *New Yorker*, 5 November 2001.

70 In a September 2013 interview with the author, a former US State Department official flatly denied the more lurid details in Seymour M. Hersh, 'Defending the Arsenal: In an Unstable Pakistan, Can Nuclear Warheads be Kept Safe?', *New Yorker*, 16 November 2009.

71 See, for example, 'Pakistan's nuclear security troubles', IHS Jane's Islamic Affairs analyst, 26 July 2011.

72 Tertrais, 'Pakistan's nuclear programme', pp. 22–23; and Sanger, *Confront and Conceal*, p. 108.

73 Shyam Saran, 'Is India's Nuclear Deterrent Credible?', speech at India Habitat Centre, New Delhi, 24 April 2013, http://krepon.armscontrolwonk.com/files/2013/05/Final-Is-Indias-Nuclear-Deterrent-Credible-rev1-2-1-3.pdf. See also Pervez Hoodbhoy, 'Pakistan: Understanding the "World's Fastest Growing Arsenal"', in Hoodbhoy (ed.), *Confronting the Bomb*, p. 97.

74 Interview with senior official, Islamabad, December 2013.

75 Schmitt and Sanger, 'In Sign of Normalization, Pentagon to Reimburse Pakistan $688 Million'.

76 Geo News TV, Karachi, 6 September 2013, via BBC Monitoring.

77 Hoodbhoy, 'Post bin Laden', p. 172.

78 Christopher Clary, 'Thinking about Pakistan's Nuclear Security in Peacetime, Crisis and War', Institute for Defence Studies and Analyses, IDSA Occasional Paper No. 12, p. 22, http://www.idsa.in/system/files/OP_PakistansNuclearSecurity.pdf.

79 *Ibid.*, p. 24.

80 Rolf Mowatt-Larssen, 'Nuclear Security in Pakistan: Reducing the

Risks of Nuclear Terrorism', *Arms Control Today*, July/August 2009.

[81] David E. Sanger, 'What to Do about Pakistan's Nuclear Arsenal?', *New York Times Magazine*, 8 January 2009.

[82] Jane Perlez, David E. Sanger and Eric Schmitt, 'Nuclear Fuel Memos Expose Wary Dance with Pakistan', *New York Times*, 30 November 2010.

[83] David Sanger and Eric Schmitt, 'Pakistani Nuclear Arms Pose Challenge to U.S. Policy', *New York Times*, 31 January 2011.

[84] Robert S. Norris and Hans M. Kristensen, 'Nuclear Notebook: Worldwide Deployments of Nuclear Weapons, 2009', *Bulletin of the Atomic Scientists*, vol. 65, no. 6, November 2009, pp. 86–98.

[85] Andrew Buncombe, 'Suicide bomber kills general in Pakistan', *Independent*, 26 February 2008, http://www.independent.co.uk/news/world/asia/suicide-bomber-kills-general-in-pakistan-787283.html.

[86] Gregory, 'The Terrorist Threat to Pakistan's Nuclear Weapons'.

[87] Jeffrey Goldberg and Marc Ambinder, 'The Ally from Hell', *The Atlantic*, December 2011; and Goldberg and Ambinder, 'Nuclear Negligence'.

[88] Author interviews in Europe and North America, 2013.

[89] Christopher Clary, 'India in Transition: Guarding the Nuclear Guardians', Center for the Advanced Study of India, 15 July 2013, http://casi.sas.upenn.edu/iit/clary.

[90] Vipin Narang, 'Five Myths about India's Nuclear Posture', *The Washington Quarterly*, vol. 36, no. 3, Summer 2013, p. 154.

[91] Prasad Sanyal, 'Karnataka terror plot: Doctor arrested in Bangalore', NDTV, 3 September 2012, http://www.ndtv.com/article/south/karnataka-terror-plot-doctor-arrested-in-bangalore-262362.

[92] Neeraj Chauhan, 'Indian Mujahideen wanted to nuke Surat, Yasin Bhatkal tells cops', *Times of India*, 30 December 2013.

[93] Lydia Dennett, 'Nuclear Site Unable to Protect Bomb Material in Recent Tests', Project on Government Oversight, 25 July 2013, http://www.pogo.org/blog/2013/07/20130725-nuclear-site-unable-to-protect-bomb-material-in-recent-tests.html.

[94] Graeme Hosken, 'Security breached', *The Times*, 12 July 2012.

[95] 'Al Baradei to Al Hayat', Dar Al Hayat, 10 January 2008, http://english.daralhayat.com/Spec/01-2008/Article-20080110-639032eb-c0a8-10ed-01ae-81ab2ea588db/story.html.

[96] 'Pakistan in Crisis: Interview with Benazir Bhutto', CNN, 5 November 2007, http://transcripts.cnn.com/TRANSCRIPTS/0711/05/sitroom.02.html; and Paul Kerr and Mary Beth Nikitin, 'Pakistan's Nuclear Weapons: Proliferation and Security Issues', Congressional Research Service, 13 February 2013, p. 16, http://www.fas.org/sgp/crs/nuke/RL34248.pdf.

[97] Moreau, 'Pakistan Insists Nukes Are Safe'.

[98] 'British Council: Pakistan facing "frightening" demographic disaster', *Telegraph*, 20 November 2009.

[99] Anatol Lieven, *Pakistan: A Hard Country* (London: Penguin Group, 2001), p. 6; Tertrais, 'Pakistan's nuclear programme', p. 25; and Jon-

athan Paris, 'Prospects for Pakistan', Legatum Institute, January 2010, p. 28, http://www.cfr.org/pakistan/legatum-institute-prospects-pakistan/p21183.

100 David Sanger, 'Pakistan Overshadows Afghanistan on US Agenda', *New York Times*, 6 May 2009.

101 Clary, 'Thinking about Pakistan's Nuclear Security in Peacetime, Crisis and War', p. 28.

102 Tertrais, 'Pakistan's nuclear programme', p. 23.

103 Author interview, Washington, October 2012.

104 'Pakistan's nuclear weapons 200% safe: Rehman Malik', *Express Tribune*, 5 June 2011, recounted in Hoodbhoy, 'Post bin Laden', p. 171.

105 Gregory, 'Terrorist Tactics in Pakistan Threaten Nuclear Weapons Safety'.

CHAPTER FIVE

The potential for onward proliferation and for nuclear accidents

A comprehensive analysis of the potential dangers associated with Pakistan's nuclear programme would not be complete without examining two other risk factors. This chapter addresses two important questions: can A.Q. Khan's transfers of nuclear-weapons technology a decade ago truly be consigned to the pages of history? And are Pakistan's nuclear facilities safe?

Onward proliferation

Pakistani officials refer to the nation's nuclear shame as the A.Q. Khan 'incident', as though it was a solitary event. In fact, Khan's transfer of his nation's nuclear-weapons technology to three aspiring nuclear-weapons states, and an offer of the same to at least one other nation, spanned over a decade. He was finally put out of business in late 2003 as a result of strong pressure from the United States, which, together with the United Kingdom, closed down his global black-market network. This lengthy period of failed nuclear stewardship continues to haunt Pakistan's international reputation and to prevent it from receiving the kind of nuclear-cooperation exemption from Nuclear Suppliers Group (NSG) guidelines accorded to India. Other nations are not convinced that onward proliferation from Pakistan will not happen again.

The saga of Khan's nuclear transfers to North Korea, Iran and Libya, and his unrequited offer to Iraq and possibly other states, has been well told.[1] Khan started as a black-market trader on behalf of the state, stealing centrifuge designs from a Urenco subsidiary and creating a loose global network to import the necessary parts to get Pakistan's enrichment programme off the ground. He transitioned to a black-market seller when, after Khan Research Laboratories (KRL) switched to P-2 model centrifuges, he realised he could make money selling the now redundant P-1 machines.

The first deal was struck in 1987 with Iranian intelligence agents through Khan's Dubai-based hub. Khan offered a menu of various weapons-related technologies and Iran paid US$3 million for several P-1 centrifuges and a list of international vendors for other equipment. Iran eventually received components for 500 P-1 centrifuges and drawings for the P-2 version. Whether the Pakistani government was involved is unclear. General Mirza Aslam Beg, chief of army staff, openly supported Iran's quest for nuclear weapons and is widely suspected of having been an accomplice, at least in terms of awareness, if not encouragement, in Khan's dealings with Tehran. Other senior Pakistani officials reportedly encouraged Khan's meetings with Iran, but no evidence has emerged that he was directed to provide the country with nuclear technology. A diffusion of political power among the troika of the president, prime minister and army chief obscured the authority over the nuclear-weapons programme and provided Khan with a relatively free rein.[2]

Khan acquired a second customer beginning in the late 1990s, when he traded gas centrifuge uranium-enrichment technology to North Korea, in exchange for more of the *Nodong* missiles that Pakistan had already begun to import. In this case, there is strong evidence that Khan was acting on behalf of the government. The 20 P-1 centrifuges and other parts that Khan sent to Pyongyang, for example, were transported in aircraft belonging to, or contracted by, the Pakistan Air Force. At a minimum, there was state complicity in terms of having knowledge of, and thereby implicitly condoning, the transfer of nuclear technology.

A third customer, Libya, initiated contacts with Khan in 1997 and began receiving shipments of P-1 centrifuges that year. The Libya deal was the most extensive and by 2003 included an order of 10,000 P-2 centrifuges and the piping system; 20 tonnes of uranium hexafluoride (UF_6); computer disks containing a full set of P-1 and P-2 centrifuge drawings; training in three continents for Libyan technical personnel; and a nearly complete design for a nuclear weapon, all at a cost of at least US$100m. Much of the equipment was never unpacked, however, and key parts of the centrifuges were never delivered. The Libya connection appeared to be an apolitical business deal between Libya and the Khan network, with no Pakistani government involvement other than acquiescence by those officials who would have noticed transfers, from Pakistan to Libya, of items such as cylinders of UF_6 that originated in North Korea.

In October 2003, the US and UK led an interdiction of the vessel *BBC China* which was en route to Libya carrying several containers of enrichment-related equipment from Khan network hubs in Malaysia and Turkey. This led Colonel Muammar Gadhafi, who had already been negotiating with the UK and US, to realise that the network had been infiltrated and that his nuclear-weapons aspirations had been fatally compromised. In December, Libya renounced its nuclear-weapons programme.

In 1990, Khan had also offered to provide Iraq with enrichment technology, materials and project designs for a nuclear bomb. Iraq did not become a fourth customer, however, because its attention was diverted by the US-led intervention in January 1991 in response to Iraq's invasion of Kuwait. Not enough is known about the offer to Iraq to make any inferences about Pakistani government involvement, but it had the appearances of a business deal, with price tags and commissions to be paid on all procurements. There is also evidence that Khan sought to market nuclear-weapons technology to Syria and possibly other countries. India has even been identified as the possible 'fourth customer' to whom the Khan network sold enrichment technology, though the evidence – a similarity of centrifuge designs and a common black-market source for some components – is thin.[3]

Khan had been under internal suspicion since the 1980s, but investigations never impinged on his onward proliferation activities because of the risks of revealing nuclear secrets and creating domestic political trouble in light of Khan's status as a national hero.[4] Pressure from the US and Khan's resistance to military oversight finally convinced President Musharraf in March 2001 to remove him as head of KRL. Yet Khan continued for two more years to pursue his dealings with Libya. Not until autumn 2003, after receiving compelling evidence from the US about Khan's illicit transfers, did Musharraf order him to be detained for thorough questioning. Khan said every army chief for two decades knew of his activities and that, if indicted, he would expose all those involved.[5] Then, and later, his story changed, but in February 2004 he was persuaded to confess publicly, taking full responsibility, after he was granted an official pardon and subjected to house arrest that has continued loosely up to the present. About 25 of his associates at KRL and elsewhere were also temporarily detained.

Neither the International Atomic Energy Agency (IAEA) nor foreign governments were allowed to talk with any of them, and certainly not Khan, lest he discredit military authorities and spill national secrets. Allowing foreign officials to question Khan would also have been politically fraught, given his domestic popularity.

Instead, the Pakistani government posed questions to Khan on behalf of the IAEA, as well as the US, UK, Japan and South Korea, all of which were pursuing investigations about Khan's associates in their own countries and elsewhere. Pakistan's assistance to global efforts to close down Khan's global network was helpful, though the answers stopped in 2006 when the government determined that the Khan interrogation was complete. Pakistan also cooperated with the IAEA's investigation of Iran's answers about its previously unreported enrichment activity, although some questions remain unanswered.[6]

Embarrassment over the Khan case prompted a reform of Pakistan's export-control legislation and a series of accountability and oversight measures in the nuclear command-and-control infrastructure. When the United Nations Security Council in 2004 adopted Resolution 1540, mandating all countries to develop effective measures to prevent illicit trafficking of sensitive nuclear materials, Pakistan dutifully reported the national measures it had taken to comply. A comprehensive export-control law that was passed in 2004 and later updated includes end-use and end-user certification and penalties for violators. In 2007 Pakistan set up a Strategic Export Control Division in the Foreign Ministry to administer export controls, and an oversight board to monitor implementation of the legislation. A national control list was established, which is meant to include items on the control lists of the NSG, the Australia Group (dealing with chemical and biological agents) and the Missile Technology Control Regime, and is periodically updated. Harmonisation with these control lists is not perfect because of a time lag in keeping up to date and because of structural problems which Pakistan is committed to overcoming. A catch-all clause to cover goods not on the control lists but that the exporter suspects may be used for a weapons purpose is weaker than the international norm. There are also some issues associated with enforcement of the regulations. As of late 2013, Pakistan had not issued a single applicable export-control licence, which suggests the need for more outreach to industry. In any case, it is doubtful that any of these measures would have applied to those aspects of the Khan transfers that were state sanctioned.

In the decade after Khan's confession and the closing down of his network there have been no further confirmed cases of illicit nuclear transfers from Pakistan.[7] In 2010, a senior US State Department official said that the Khan network was 'basically defunct'.[8] In light of the reforms that have been adopted, it is reasonable to consider if and when Pakistan can be considered to be rehabilitated. Concerns still remain, however, that Pakistan might transfer nuclear weapons as a matter of national policy.

Nuclear transfer to Saudi Arabia?

In November 2013, a BBC report recycled long-standing claims that Pakistan was ready to provide nuclear weapons to Saudi Arabia in exchange for the financing Riyadh had provided to Pakistan's nuclear programme for over three decades.[9] In recent years, Saudi officials have repeatedly indicated that if rival Iran developed nuclear weapons, the kingdom would have to acquire a nuclear equaliser of its own. Because a domestic nuclear-weapons programme could not be developed in time to catch up, it is often assumed that if Saudi Arabia decided on a nuclear option, it would ask Pakistan to provide off-the-shelf weapons.

Given their disillusionment over Washington's withdrawal of support for President Hosni Mubarak in Egypt, failure to follow through on a stated intention to strike Bashar al-Assad in Syria, and nuclear negotiations that would likely leave Iran with a weapons capability, the Saudis may well believe that it is time to turn to Pakistan. Details about the understanding between the two countries in the 1990s remain unclear, but it reportedly involved a promise to provide nuclear assistance if Saudi Arabia faced dire circumstances. This might have meant nuclear protection akin to the nuclear umbrella the United States provides to its allies, with or without Pakistani nuclear forces deployed in the kingdom. There are strong reasons to doubt that Pakistan would turn over nuclear weapons to Saudi Arabia, given strategic, economic and diplomatic disincentives. In a comprehensive review of the costs and benefits of doing so, former US defence department official Colin Kahl and fellow authors at the Center for New American Security assessed in 2013 that 'the transfer of operational nuclear weapons to Saudi Arabia would likely be seen as one of the most provocative transactions in history.'[10] Pakistan would face new sanctions, including the probable loss of US$2 billion annual US aid, and would lose any prospect of ever being given a nuclear-cooperation exemption like the one accorded to India. Such a transaction would create a new security dilemma for Pakistan on its western front with Iran and exacerbate domestic Sunni–Shiite troubles while aggravating Pakistan's strategic balance with India by reducing Pakistan's nuclear arsenal.

As with previous similar media reports, the Pakistan Foreign Ministry called the BBC exposé 'speculative, mischievous and baseless'.[11] In light of the multiple sourcing in the story and the amount of evidence that has accumulated over the years about the Saudi–Pakistan deal, that denial is too sweeping. On balance, however, a transfer of nuclear weapons is highly unlikely. More feasible is technical assistance by retired Pakistani nuclear scientists.

Nuclear safety risks

An assessment of the risks that arise from Pakistan's nuclear programmes must also address the potential for nuclear accidents. Chapter Three touched upon the ways in which battlefield-use weapons pose a greater risk of accidental detonation if their shorter range requires mating and transport under crisis conditions. Not just the newer, short-range models, but all of Pakistan's nuclear weapons, as well as India's, are inherently less safe than those of the five NPT-recognised nuclear-weapons states because of the small number of hot tests conducted by the South Asian states. As Zia Mian warns, 'this may make it unlikely that they have incorporated either insensitive high explosives or fire resistant pits as safety features. If they are deployed, there may be a risk of accidental detonation.'[12] US weapons, for example, were tested 62 times to ensure they are 'one-point safe'. This means that when the high explosives surrounding the pit are detonated at any single point, 'the probability of producing a nuclear yield exceeding the force of the explosives is less than one in a million.'[13] Because Pakistan's warheads are not one-point safe, a nuclear explosion cannot be ruled out if one is hit with a conventional bomb, although more likely would be a dirty-bomb-like dispersal of radiation.

Accidents can be caused by fires, sabotage and crashes of the aircraft or trucks that transport the weapons, among other causes. As the numbers of weapons and weapons systems increase, the ways that accidents can occur expand as well. Investigative journalist Eric Schlosser recently chronicled the

32 accidents involving nuclear weapons that the United States experienced between 1950 and 1980.[14]

The Pakistani government pays serious attention to nuclear safety. It is a signatory to the Convention on Nuclear Safety and follows international nuclear safety standards. Absorbing lessons from the Fukushima nuclear disaster, the Pakistan Atomic Energy Commission (PAEC) identified a comprehensive set of safety retrofits, its chairman said in 2012.[15] Pakistan's 'nuclear safety and security action plan', initiated in 2006, reportedly has been called a model for other states.[16] Being a non-party to the NPT does not hinder cooperation with the IAEA in nuclear safety and security. Over 200 Pakistani specialists have attended IAEA training courses. An emergency-response team analogous to the US Nuclear Emergency Search Team is also in place to enhance safety and security of both civilian and military nuclear facilities.

Nuclear accidents can never be ruled out entirely, of course. Even apart from the risk of a terrorist attack, there are several reasons to worry about radiation emissions in Pakistan. The age and siting of the Karachi Nuclear Power Plant (KANUPP), for example, raise concerns. When built in 1972, the small power plant had a design life of 30 years. With assistance from Canada, a relicensing process extended the lifespan to 2019, but critics wonder if this was worthwhile, given the small amount of electricity the plant produces.[17] KANUPP is 20km upwind from the centre of the nation's largest city, whose population has expanded six-fold, to over 21m, since the plant was built. No reactor anywhere else in the world potentially endangers more people.[18]

Critics also fault the newer Chashma reactors, located on the banks of the Indus River, the nation's lifeline, and in a seismic zone. Some also question the desirability, on safety grounds, of relying entirely on China for nuclear cooperation, as dictated by Pakistan's rejection by the other members of the NSG. Chashma-1 was based on China's first indigenous reactor, Qinshan-1, which experienced design problems. Although Qinshan used reliable Western and Japanese components, China had to build everything for Chashma itself.[19] The newer Chashma reactors are also based on the old design, which incorporated fewer safety features than later Chinese reactors.[20] The new reactors to be built at Karachi are based on a new design that is still under development in China. Pakistani critics of the project contend that since the new reactors will be the first of a kind, it is unclear how safe they will be. They also note that as of December 2013, there had been no public hearings or discussions on the environmental suitability of the site for the new reactors.[21]

Some critics also contend that Pakistan lacks a safety culture. In Pervez Hoodbhoy's words, 'whether driving cars or running nuclear plants, Pakistanis are risk-takers looking for shortcuts, choosing to put their faith in God rather than precautions.'[22] Exaggerated though this criticism may be, it has a ring of truth.

The picture is thus mixed. On one hand, Pakistan follows international safety standards in matters such as transport of civilian nuclear material, and presumably applies even more controls in the military nuclear sector. On the other hand, if even Japan, with its advanced technology and safety culture, could experience a disaster on the scale of Fukushima, it is hard to be sanguine about nuclear safety in Pakistan.

Notes

1   See, for example, IISS, *Nuclear Black Markets: Pakistan, A.Q. Khan and the rise of proliferation networks – A net assessment* (London: IISS, 2007), pp. 65–105.

2   *Ibid.*, pp. 69–70.

3   Joshua Pollack, 'The Secret Treachery of A.Q. Khan', *Playboy*, January/February 2012.

4   IISS, *Nuclear Black Markets*, pp. 94–96.

5   *Ibid.*, p. 98.

6   *Ibid.*, p. 102.

7   In 2007, reports surfaced of Pakistani citizens being involved with sales of nuclear- or missile-related goods to countries of proliferation concern, but these cases were never confirmed. IISS, *Nuclear Black Markets*, p. 117.

8   'Transshipment And Diversion: Are U.S. Trading Partners Doing Enough To Prevent The Spread Of Dangerous Technologies?', Hearing of the Terrorism, Nonproliferation and Trade Subcommittee of the House Foreign Affairs Committee, 22 July 2010, http://www.gpo.gov/fdsys/pkg/CHRG-111hhrg57609/html/CHRG-111hhrg57609.htm.

9   Mark Urban, 'Saudi nuclear weapons "on order" from Pakistan', BBC News, 6 November 2013, http://www.bbc.co.uk/news/world-middle-east-24823846.

10 Colin H. Kahl, Melissa G. Dalton and Matthew Irvine, 'Atomic Kingdom: If Iran Builds the Bomb, Will Saudi Arabia Be Next?', Center for a New American Security, February 2013, p. 26, http://www.cnas.org/files/documents/publications/CNAS_AtomicKingdom_Kahl.pdf.

11 Urban, 'Saudi nuclear weapons "on order" from Pakistan'.

12 Zia Mian, 'Commanding and Controlling Nuclear Weapons', in Pervez Hoodbhoy (ed.), *Confronting the Bomb: Pakistani and Indian Scientists Speak Out* (Karachi: Oxford University Press, 2013), p. 227.

13 Ashton Carter, John D. Steinbruner, and Charles A. Zraket, *Managing Nuclear Operations* (Washington DC: Brookings Institution Press, 1987), p. 43. Only in a controlled nuclear firing would there be a simultaneous ignition of the explosives at more than one point.

14 Eric Schlosser, *Command and Control: Nuclear Weapons, the Damascus Accident, and the Illusion of Safety* (London: Penguin Press, 2013).

15 'Purchase of Safety-Related Nuclear Equipment: Pakistan Slams Curbs by Some Countries', *Dawn*, 19 September 2012.

16 'Nuclear facilities are safe, says Pakistan', *The Nation*, 7 November 2012.

17 Rina Saeed Khan, 'Underpowered and unsafe, Pakistan's nuclear reactors are just big boys' toys', *Guardian*, 28 April 2011.

18 Declan Butler, 'Reactors, residents and risk', *Nature*, 21 April 2011, http://www.nature.com/news/2011/110421/full/472400a.html.

19 Zia Mian and A.H. Nayyar, 'Pakistan's Chashma Nuclear Power Plant: A preliminary study of some safety issues and estimates of the consequences of a severe accident', Center for Energy and Environmental Studies, Princeton University, Report No. 321, December 1999, http://www.princeton.edu/sgs/publications/center-reports/CEES-321%20revised.pdf.

20 Chris Buckley, 'China pushes ahead Pakistan nuclear plant expansion', Reuters, 24 March 2011, http://in.reuters.com/article/2011/03/24/idINIndia-55836320110324.

21 A.H. Nayyar, Pervez Hoodbhoy and Zia Mian, 'Nuclear Karachi', *Dawn*, 16 December 2013.

22 Pervez Hoodbhoy, 'Pakistan can't handle Fukushima', *Express Tribune*, 22 March 2011.

What began as a civilian nuclear programme in Pakistan in the mid-1950s took on a military dimension even before suspicions were confirmed that India was on a nuclear-weapons path. As remains the case today, Pakistan assumed the worst about India's intentions and spared no effort in preparing a nuclear counterpunch. By 1983, just 11 years after receiving orders to produce a nuclear weapon, Pakistani scientists carried out the first cold test of a nuclear device. Hot tests in 1998 confirmed that the highly enriched uranium-based weapons indeed worked. Pakistan subsequently developed plutonium-based weapons and nine different ballistic- and cruise-missile systems to supplement the aircraft-delivery means.

Although the figures are notional, Pakistan in 2014 is esti-mated to have about 110–130 weapons. It produces highly enriched uranium sufficient for about six bombs per year and plutonium for about four more bombs. The recent addition of two more plutonium-production reactors means that by 2016, Pakistan may be able to produce about 16 bombs per year. Although India has more nuclear facilities and a larger stock-pile of spent fuel that could be put to weapons use, Pakistan's atomic-bomb arsenal is growing faster than that of any other country. By the mid-2020s, it could be the world's fifth or even fourth largest, ahead of both France and the UK. While Pakistan continues to advocate 'minimum credible deterrence', the emphasis is on credibility rather than minimalism. Nuclear weapons are a way to equalise India's growing superiority in military spending and conventional weaponry. Plutonium production was further spurred in the new millennium by threat perceptions concerning Indian Army mobilisation plans and the US–India nuclear-cooperation deal that disadvantages Pakistan both strategically and psychologically.

Constrained by limited uranium sources, Pakistan's arsenal will not grow inexorably. If the strategic environment is stable, senior military officials say production could stop by 2020. By then, Pakistan might have 200 or so weapons. Meanwhile, Pakistan, like India, continues to expand its delivery systems. Of gravest concern is the recent introduction of short-range ballistic-missile systems – the 60km-range *Nasr* and the 180km-range *Abdali*. Pakistan describes them as giving it a tactical and theatre-level capability to supplement its strategic deterrence. It speaks of needing these tactical nuclear weapons (TNWs) to 'plug the deterrence gap' – that is, to deny India the space for military operations below Pakistan's perceived nuclear threshold. The *Nasr*, in particular, is a response to the Indian Army's aspirational 'Cold Start' plan to launch a conventional incursion to deter terrorist attacks emanating from Pakistan. The fact that India's civilian leadership has never endorsed Cold Start makes it no less threatening in Pakistani eyes. But realising that TNWs cannot actually stop an enemy tank offensive, Pakistani military planners say their role is purely for deterrence, not for actual use in a war.

This lowering of the nuclear threshold to include non-existential threats could lead to a devastating nuclear exchange.

Since their independence in 1945, India and Pakistan have warred three times. In the last 28 years they have nearly gone to war five other times, including the 2001–02 crisis that prompted diplomats to evacuate. The presence of nuclear weapons contributed to calming those crises, but in an example of the 'stability/instability' paradox, those weapons have also encouraged risk taking. Abetted by accidents, misperceptions or miscalculation, there remains a grave concern that another large-scale terrorist attack in India with Pakistani state fingerprints could trigger nuclear use. The development of cruise missiles, sea-based platforms and other ambiguous dual-use systems heightens the potential for misperception. The underdeveloped mechanisms for crisis resolution in South Asia and the absence of dialogue on the factors behind nuclear risks are further reasons for concern.

The gravest nuclear danger concerning Pakistan is the intensifying nuclear-arms competition. In terms of numbers and the avoidance to date of a hair-trigger alert status, the competition pales in comparison to the US–Soviet rivalry. One worrisome difference, however, is the sense of nonchalance exhibited in South Asia about the dangers of nuclear war. The nuclear competition there is also largely unidirectional, as India seeks to catch up with China and Pakistan tries to match India, albeit not in every respect. While Pakistan is increasing its nuclear-weapons arsenal at a faster pace, India has far more potential for ramping up – a situation that feeds Pakistan's worst-case assumptions. Asymmetries also govern the two sides' nuclear doctrines. India foreswears first use of nuclear weapons but vows massive retaliation in response to a nuclear attack, even if against Indian forces operating outside national borders. Pakistan threatens to use battlefield nuclear weapons in response to conventional attacks that would not pose an existential threat. The credibility of both doctrines can be questioned but not ignored.

The potentially destabilising impact of a nuclear arms race in South Asia is exacerbated by Pakistan's introduction of battlefield nuclear weapons. Due to the 'use them or lose them' choice that could face local commanders, deployment of these systems can lead to rapid escalation if deterrence fails. Pakistan's need to portray credibility about firing first could sacrifice central government control over strategic weapons in a crisis situation. Pre-delegation can lead to unauthorised use. These are some of the reasons that NATO moved away from TNWs, which were found to be a costly encumbrance with little practical value. Pakistan insists that its TNWs will not be pre-deployed nor will use be delegated to field commanders. In the fog of a crisis, however, even the most robust of command-and-control systems cannot preclude human error.

The South Asian nuclear competition has hampered global arms-control efforts, particularly the quest for a Fissile Material Cut-off Treaty (FMCT). Seeing the FMCT as directed primarily against its interests, Pakistan, since 2009, has single-handedly blocked any discussion of the matter at the Geneva-based Conference on Disarmament. It insists its veto will not be lifted until it is accorded nuclear cooperation akin to the deal that India was granted. It would seem, however, that a treaty that capped relatively equal fissile-material stockpiles and prevented India from reprocessing its civilian spent fuel for weapons use could be to Pakistan's advantage. The arms competition also makes India and Pakistan less interested in joining the Comprehensive Nuclear-Test-Ban Treaty (CTBT), which cannot come into force until they and six other hold-outs, including China and the United States, ratify the treaty. For Pakistan, signing the CTBT could offer diplomatic advantages, depending on the deal it could strike.

As discussed in Chapter Four, the potential for nuclear terrorism is the nuclear danger most commonly associated with Pakistan. This is not without reason, given the number and brazenness of extremists in the country and the creeping fundamentalism that exacerbates concerns about insider collusion. The more weapons and fissile material that are produced, the more potential there is for theft, seizure or sabotage, especially when materials are in transit. The threat is often exaggerated, however. Four terrorist groups in Pakistan have reportedly expressed interest in nuclear weapons, but their inclinations tend to be opportunistic. Six terrorist attacks have occurred at military facilities that reportedly house nuclear assets but not necessarily because of those assets, which were never in danger. A fundamentalist takeover of the country is highly unlikely given the cohesion and discipline of the army and the esteem in which it is held.

While the prospect of nuclear terrorism cannot be dismissed, there is insufficient recognition of the steps Pakistan has taken to protect its nuclear programme. The Strategic Plans Division's (SPD) four-tier approach – physical protection, human-reliability programmes, an emergency management system and comprehensive training – is not perfect. Security controls such as permissive action links (the sophisticated locks designed to prevent accidental or unauthorised launching of nuclear weapons) can be circumvented, for example, especially if priority is given to launch reliability. Yet it is fair to say that no country devotes more attention to nuclear security, and Pakistan quietly cooperates with Western partners. But national paranoia about US intentions undermines some of these efforts, for example when nuclear weapons are moved more frequently as a precaution against a supposed American conspiracy. Contrary to popular belief in Pakistan, the May 2011 US raid on Osama bin Laden's compound was not a practice run for seizing the nation's nuclear weapons, which in any case are too well dispersed and defended for any such fanciful plan to succeed. Only if a nuclear-weapons cache were under threat of falling into terrorist hands would the US consider intervening.

The danger of onward proliferation appears to have receded after the detention of black marketeer A.Q. Khan in late 2003 and the reforms Pakistan put in place governing its nuclear programme. Khan's nuclear sales to North Korea, Iran and Libya from 1987 to 2003, and offers to Iraq and possibly other countries stained Pakistan's reputation in ways that continue to reverberate, preventing it from obtaining a nuclear-cooperation exemption from Nuclear Suppliers Group (NSG) guidelines similar to India's, for example. Pakistan's export controls continue to improve, though questions are still asked as to whether Pakistan might transfer nuclear weapons to Saudi Arabia as a matter of national policy. In past decades, Riyadh reportedly helped to fund Pakistan's nuclear programme in exchange for a promise of nuclear assistance if needed. Today, Saudi Arabian sources talk frankly about possibly needing to counter Iran's nuclear capabilities and there are recurrent press reports about the kingdom seeking weapons or development assistance from Pakistan. Yet the strategic, economic and diplomatic disincentives for Pakistan to carry out such requests make a nuclear transfer unlikely.

Rounding out the risks that arise from Pakistan's nuclear programme is the potential for nuclear accidents in both the military and civilian nuclear realms. Due to the small number of tests they have conducted, one can deduce that the nuclear weapons possessed by both Pakistan and India are less safe than those of the five NPT-recognised nuclear-weapons states. If deployed, there is a risk of accidental detonation, including if hit by enemy artillery. As the history of the US atomic-weapons programme demonstrates, accidents can also happen for many other reasons. In the civilian sector, Pakistan pays serious attention to nuclear safety, but there are reasons for concern about the design and siting of its reactors.

Nuclear normalisation

Reducing the dangers associated with Pakistan's nuclear programme will require the country and its international partners to make mutually reinforcing adjustments. Pakistan should be treated as a normal nuclear country if it adopts policies and practices associated with global nuclear norms.

For nuclear-armed states, nuclear norms can be considered in terms of: firstly, restraint in declaratory policy; secondly, practices that ensure safety and security; and thirdly, institutional compliance with the global non-proliferation regime. Pointing to many examples, Pakistani officials insist that their nation is a responsible nuclear-weapons state. The nation's performance in some areas is certainly beyond reproach. In other areas, however, it does not meet the norm. Depending on which indicators are deemed most relevant, most other nuclear states fall short as well, of course. Pakistan bears a heavier burden of proof, however, because of the failure of nuclear stewardship regarding transfers by the A.Q. Khan network and because of the ongoing threats posed by other non-state actors in Pakistan.[1]

With regard to restraint in declaratory policies, Pakistan, like other nations possessing nuclear weapons, holds that they are strictly for defensive purposes. Pakistan also states that the weapons are for deterrence and only for war-fighting if deterrence breaks down. Pakistan's stated policies of minimum deterrence and no pre-delegation of launch authority are further indicators of nuclear responsibility, as is its unofficial policy of keeping warheads and delivery systems de-mated, and thus on a low level of alert status. Pakistan's proposals for a bilateral nuclear restraint regime with India are also a positive step. It is questionable, however, whether Pakistan adheres to minimalism any longer, given the expansion of its plutonium-production facilities, warhead numbers and delivery systems, and the introduction of battlefield-use nuclear weapons. The policy most at odds with what is commonly seen as responsible nuclear behaviour is Pakistan's declared doctrine of nuclear use in response to a conventional military incursion that does not threaten the integrity of the state. This lowering of the threshold for nuclear use is the gravest concern.

In the second area of nuclear norms, Pakistan deserves more credit than the nation is commonly accorded for its adherence to practices that ensure safety and security of nuclear arsenals and material throughout the fuel cycle. Pakistan understands the danger of nuclear terrorism and has done much to reduce vulnerabilities. The country has played a prominent role in the Nuclear Security Summit process over the past four years. To further strengthen nuclear-security practices, Pakistan should sign and ratify the International Convention for the Suppression of Acts of Nuclear Terrorism and ratify the 2005 amendment to the Convention on the Physical Protection of Nuclear Material.

Pakistan adheres to most international norms of nuclear safety. The main problem in this area is the state's inability to control the terrorists that operate from its territory. Nuclear terrorism in its usual sense means terrorist attacks on nuclear facilities or seizure of nuclear assets. A greater danger of nuclear terrorism in the wider sense is the potential for extremists sparking a nuclear war by conducting spectacular terrorist attacks in India.

The third area – compliance with the global non-proliferation regime – presents the most obvious examples of where Pakistan is outside the mainstream. As long as it retains nuclear weapons, Pakistan will never be a party to the NPT, which for a host of practical reasons cannot be amended. There is no similar structural impediment to joining the CTBT or to allowing negotiation of an FMCT. On the positive side, Pakistan is a member in good standing of the International Atomic Energy Agency (IAEA) and has put all of its civilian nuclear facilities under safeguards. It has a robust export-control system and a multi-tiered set of arrangements to ensure against repetition of onward proliferation by non-state actors.

Seeking to join the four multilateral export-control regimes, Pakistan has initiated dialogue with the NSG, the Missile Technology Control Regime, the Australia Group and the Wassenaar Arrangement (for conventional weapons). Above all, Pakistan demands to be treated on par with India in being granted an exception to NSG rules and national policies against nuclear cooperation with non-NPT parties.

The exception for India came about mainly for geostrategic reasons. Under President George W. Bush, the United States saw it as a means of bolstering India as a bulwark against China. Out of deference to political and diplomatic sensitivities, that rationale went largely unspoken. Instead, the exception was justified on the grounds of India's proclaimed nuclear responsibility. Although India's non-proliferation record was not as perfect as claimed,[2] it stood in sharp contrast to Pakistan's failure to stop Khan's nuclear sales. When the US–India nuclear-cooperation agreement was first announced in July 2005, those proliferation transfers were a very recent memory, with Khan having been put out of business only the year before.

Ten years after Khan's network was shut down, it is fair to ask how long Pakistan must pay the price for that failure. Over the past decade, US policy, which once tilted toward Pakistan and after the Cold War sought to strike a balance between the two South Asian powers, has shifted decidedly in favour of India. Meanwhile, Pakistan's estrangement from the West feeds the negative dynamic of growing fundamentalist tendencies in Pakistani society.

The time has come to offer Pakistan a nuclear-cooperation deal akin to India's. Providing a formula for nuclear normalisation is the most powerful tool that Western countries can wield in positively shaping Pakistan's nuclear posture. Offering nuclear legitimacy is also the most effective way to communicate that the United States and its allies do not seek to forcefully or stealthily disarm Pakistan, and that the Western goal, rather, is deterrence stability.

In a persuasive 2011 report, nuclear experts at the Washington-based Carnegie Endowment for International Peace argued that rather than carving out another exception to the NSG rules, Pakistan's interests and those of the supplier states would be better served by adjusting the rules. A criteria-based approach for nuclear cooperation with states outside the NPT makes good sense. The Carnegie report offered its concept of additional framework criteria in four categories, which would apply both to nuclear cooperation and to NSG membership.[3]

Pakistan has already met most of the minimalist conditions required of India, including separating military and civilian facilities, putting the latter under safeguards, seeking to harmonise strategic trade controls with the export-control regimes and continuing a nuclear testing moratorium. For India, the formula also included support for FMCT negotiations. At a bare minimum, Pakistan would have to end its veto over initiating FMCT talks in Geneva.

Given that Pakistan has more to atone for and cannot match the strategic benefit that India's nuclear normalisation seemed to offer,[4] the quid pro quo would necessarily include some different terms. Pakistan should also be asked to end fissile-material production, as each of the nuclear-weapons states acknowledged by the NPT are thought to have done, although in China's case this has not been confirmed. It may be unrealistic to expect Pakistan today to stop plutonium production and separation, but by the time an FMCT is negotiated and ratified by other key states, Pakistan may already have enough plutonium to meet its military requirements.

In the meantime, NSG members should be wary of preferentially accepting India's application for membership. Doing so would likely drive Pakistan further away from the West and make it harder in the future to devise criteria that would enable Pakistani membership, over which India would then have a veto. In any case, NSG membership should be based on equitable criteria, not exceptions.

Pakistan should also be asked to lock in its testing moratorium by signing and ratifying the CTBT. Although it is commonly assumed that domestic politics would not permit Pakistan to take this or any other arms-control step in advance of India doing so, there would be diplomatic benefits in getting the jump on New Delhi, especially if this were the price for admission into the international nuclear order.

Countering groups that employ terrorism against India is another important action Pakistan could take to reduce nuclear dangers. When such concerns are raised, Pakistanis often point to counterclaims of Indian support for terrorist acts in Balochistan and elsewhere in Pakistan.[5] Regardless of the validity of such claims, a finger-pointing response misses the point. Terrorist attacks anywhere are certainly reprehensible, particularly when they are directed against one country by groups with links to government elements of a second country. Large-scale terrorist attacks against India by Pakistan-based radicals are more invidious because they could spark a conflict leading to nuclear war. As George Perkovich persuasively argues, deterrence stability requires Pakistan to restore the state monopoly on force.[6] Violence against India such as the 2001 and 2008 attacks must be delegitimised by incarcerating leaders of terrorist groups and putting those groups that operate from Pakistan out of business. That is no easy task, of course. Pakistan must at least cease its support for groups that conduct terrorism, regardless of the nationality of their targets. At the same time, India must realise that Pakistan does not control all groups that perpetrate terrorism.

Above all, India and Pakistan should find a way to engage one another on the issues that could spark a nuclear clash. Deterrence stability and the factors that contribute to growing nuclear risks should be central topics of dialogue, covering both conventional and nuclear forces. Given the dynamics that could lead to nuclear use, walling off nuclear dialogue from discussions on conventional arms makes no sense. Alleviating the arms race is a worthy goal for the new governments that are likely to be in place in both countries by mid-2014.

Notes

[1] William Harris, *Nuclear responsibility and nuclear trade: international rules and institutions to manage nuclear fuel cycles* (Santa Monica, CA: RAND, 1977). The current author is indebted to Dr Nicola Horsburgh for sharing her assessment of the concept of responsible nuclear behaviour.

[2] David Albright and Susan Basu, 'Neither a Determined Proliferator Nor a Responsible Nuclear State: India's Record Needs Scrutiny', Institute for Science and International Security, 5 April 2006, http://www.nci.org/06nci/04/indiacritique.pdf.

[3] Toby Dalton, Mark Hibbs and George Perkovich, 'A Criteria-Based Approach to Nuclear Cooperation With Pakistan', Carnegie Endowment for International Peace, Policy Outlook, 22 June 2011, http://carnegieendowment.org/2011/06/22/criteria-based-approach-to-nuclear-cooperation-with-pakistan/dt.

[4] The strategic benefits that Pakistan provided in the past in assisting with ousting the Soviet Union from Afghanistan and more recently with counter-terrorism campaigns deserve appreciation, but have a depreciated current value.

5 See, for example, Umar Cheema, 'Ex-Indian Army chief admits sponsoring terrorism in Balochistan', *News International*, 21 October 2013.

6 George Perkovich, 'Non-unitary model and deterrence stability in South Asia', Stimson Center, 13 November 2012, http://carnegie endowment.org/2012/11/13/ non-unitary-model-and-deterrence-stability-in-south-asia/ eihm.

INDEX

Adelphi books are published eight times a year by Routledge Journals, an imprint of Taylor & Francis, 4 Park Square, Milton Park, Abingdon, Oxfordshire OX14 4RN, UK.

A subscription to the institution print edition, ISSN 1944-5571, includes free access for any number of concurrent users across a local area network to the online edition, ISSN 1944-558X. Taylor & Francis has a flexible approach to subscriptions enabling us to match individual libraries' requirements. This journal is available via a traditional institutional subscription (either print with free online access, or online-only at a discount) or as part of the Strategic, Defence and Security Studies subject package or Strategic, Defence and Security Studies full text package. For more information on our sales packages please visit www.tandfonline.com/librarians_pricinginfo_journals.

2014 Annual Adelphi Subscription Rates			
Institution	£585	$1,028 USD	€865
Individual	£207	$353 USD	€282
Online only	£512	$899 USD	€758

Dollar rates apply to subscribers outside Europe. Euro rates apply to all subscribers in Europe except the UK and the Republic of Ireland where the pound sterling price applies. All subscriptions are payable in advance and all rates include postage. Journals are sent by air to the USA, Canada, Mexico, India, Japan and Australasia. Subscriptions are entered on an annual basis, i.e. January to December. Payment may be made by sterling cheque, dollar cheque, international money order, National Giro, or credit card (Amex, Visa, Mastercard).

For a complete and up-to-date guide to Taylor & Francis journals and books publishing programmes, and details of advertising in our journals, visit our website: http://www.tandfonline.com.

Ordering information:
USA/Canada: Taylor & Francis Inc., Journals Department, 325 Chestnut Street, 8th Floor, Philadelphia, PA 19106, USA. UK/Europe/Rest of World: Routledge Journals, T&F Customer Services, T&F Informa UK Ltd., Sheepen Place, Colchester, Essex, CO3 3LP, UK.

Advertising enquiries to:
USA/Canada: The Advertising Manager, Taylor & Francis Inc., 325 Chestnut Street, 8th Floor, Philadelphia, PA 19106, USA. Tel: +1 (800) 354 1420. Fax: +1 (215) 625 2940. UK/Europe/Rest of World: The Advertising Manager, Routledge Journals, Taylor & Francis, 4 Park Square, Milton Park, Abingdon, Oxfordshire OX14 4RN, UK. Tel: +44 (0) 20 7017 6000. Fax: +44 (0) 20 7017 6336.

The print edition of this journal is printed on ANSI conforming acid-free paper by Bell & Bain, Glasgow, UK.